Copyright © 2023 by Sophia M. Johnson (Author)

All rights reserved. This book or any portion thereof may not be reproduced or used in any manner whatsoever without the express written permission of the publisher except for the use of brief quotations in a book review.

This book is copyright protected. This is only for personal use. You cannot amend, distributor, sell, use, quote or paraphrase any part or the content within this book without the consent of the author.

Please note the information contained within this document is for educational and entertainment purposes only. Every attempt has been made to provide accurate, up to date and reliable complete information. No warranties of any kind are expressed or implied. Readers acknowledge that the author is not engaging in the rendering of legal, financial, medical or professional advice. The content of this book has been derived from various sources. Please consult a licensed professional before attempting any techniques outlined in this book.

By reading this document, the readers agree that under no circumstances are the author responsible for any losses, direct or indirect, which are incurred as a result of the use of information contained within this document, including but not limited to errors, omissions or inaccuracies.

Thank you very much for reading this book.

*Title: Silver Screen Legends*
*Subtitle: The Inside Story of 10 Iconic NFL Movies That Changed Football and Cinema*


Author: Sophia M. Johnson

## Table of Contents

**Introduction** .................................................................. **6**
*The Evolution of Football's Presence on the Silver Screen* ........ 6
*Choosing the 10 Most Iconic Films About the NFL* .................. 10
*Themes and Comparisons to Be Explored* ............................. 14
**Chapter 1: The Longest Yard (1974)** ........................... **18**
*The Inspiration: Movies Set in Prison* .................................... 18
*Burt Reynolds Cements His Star Status* ................................ 22
*Critically Acclaimed, Commercially Successful* ...................... 27
*Depictions of Masculinity and Rebellion* ................................ 33
**Chapter 2: North Dallas Forty (1979)** ........................ **41**
*Pulling Back the Curtain on Pro Football* ............................... 41
*Nick Nolte's Breakthrough Role* ........................................... 47
*Mature Themes Explore Football's Toll* ................................. 54
*The Lingering Impact on Sports Dramas* ............................... 60
**Chapter 3: Brian's Song (1971)** .................................. **67**
*The Tearjerker That Caught the NFL By Surprise* .................. 67
*Unlikely Friendship Between Sayers and Piccolo* ................... 72
*Breaking Barriers On and Off the Field* ................................. 78
*New Perspective on Black Athletes* ...................................... 84
**Chapter 4: Rudy (1993)** .............................................. **90**
*Bringing Rudy Ruettiger's Inspirational Story to the Big Screen* ............................................................................... 90
*Sean Astin's Breakout Dramatic Performance* ....................... 96
*The Appeal of the Ultimate Underdog Tale* .......................... 101
*Questioning the Truth Behind the Legend* ........................... 107
**Chapter 5: The Replacements (2000)** ...................... **113**
*Capitalizing on the 1987 Players' Strike* ............................... 113
*Building a Comedic Story Around Replacement Players* ...... 120
*Keanu Reeves as the Ragtag Team's Leader* ....................... 127

*Suspension of Disbelief Required* .............................................*134*

**Chapter 6: Any Given Sunday (1999)**....................... **141**
*Oliver Stone's Hyperkinetic Football Epic* ............................. *141*
*Al Pacino Commands as a Beleaguered Coach*.................... *147*
*Exposing the Brutality Behind the Glamor*............................. *153*
*Stone's Theatrical Flourishes Energize Familiar Tropes* ...... *158*

**Chapter 7: The Blind Side (2009)** ........................... **163**
*Bringing Michael Oher's Life to the Screen*............................*163*
*Sandra Bullock's Oscar-Winning Performance*....................*168*
*Feel-Good True Story Appeals to Wide Audience* .................. *173*
*Racial and Economic Issues Simmer Beneath Uplifting Tale*
.............................................................................................*178*

**Chapter 8: Invincible (2006)** .................................. **183**
*Vince Papale's Improbable NFL Dream Comes True* ...........*183*
*Mark Wahlberg Anchors Disney Sports Drama* ...................*188*
*Lean and Formulaic Retelling of Real-Life Miracle Season*..*193*
*Philadelphia Eagles' Claim to Underdog Lore*.......................*198*

**Chapter 9: Jerry Maguire (1996)**........................... **203**
*Show Me the Money: The Origins of a Modern Catchphrase*
............................................................................................. *203*
*Tom Cruise at His Charismatic Peak* ....................................*208*
*Dramedy Balance Earns Widespread Appeal* .......................*213*
*Lasting Cultural Impact Beyond Football* .............................*219*

**Chapter 10: Draft Day (2014)** ................................**224**
*Pulling Back the Curtain on the NFL Draft*.......................... *224*
*Kevin Costner Leads Ensemble Cast* ................................... *229*
*More Character Study Than Hard-Hitting Drama*.............. *234*
*Piggybacking on Real Draft Intrigue*.................................... *239*

**Chapter 11: Themes and Comparisons Across the Films**
............................................................................................**245**
*Shifting Portrayals of Race Relations*................................... *245*

*Football as an Allegory for Life's Lessons* ............................. 250
*Critiques of Commercialization and Culture* ......................... 254
*New Styles and Perspectives in Sports Films* ........................ 258
**Chapter 12: NFL Films' Impact on Wider Culture....262**
*Catchphrases, Memorable Characters, and Moments* .......... 262
*Reinforcing and Challenging Stereotypes* ............................. 265
*Tangible Influences on Generations of Fans* ......................... 268
**Conclusion..............................................................................272**
*The Definitive 10 - Ranking the Most Important NFL Films* 272
*Lingering Questions and Avenues for Future Study* .............. 277
*The Ever-Expanding Relationship of Film and Football*........ 281
**Glossary................................................................................. 286**
**Potential References ................................................. 289**

# Introduction
## The Evolution of Football's Presence on the Silver Screen

In the ever-evolving tapestry of cinematic storytelling, few subjects captivate audiences with the same visceral intensity as the collision of bodies on the football field. Over the decades, football has become more than just a sport—it's a cultural phenomenon, a narrative vehicle that transcends the boundaries of the gridiron to illuminate the human condition. In this exploration, we embark on a journey through the annals of cinema, dissecting the symbiotic relationship between football and the silver screen.

The roots of football's cinematic presence delve into the early days of filmmaking, where rudimentary cameras captured the essence of the game in its nascent form. Yet, it wasn't until the mid-20th century that football truly found its stride in the world of cinema. As the sport solidified its place in American hearts, filmmakers recognized the potential of football as a dynamic backdrop for compelling narratives that extend far beyond the confines of the playing field.

With this realization came a surge of football-themed movies that sought to capture the essence of the game, exploring its multifaceted impact on society, culture, and individual lives. The journey kicks off with classics like "The Longest Yard" (1974), where the gridiron becomes a metaphorical battleground for rebellion, and the cinematic journey unfolds, offering a lens into the complex and often turbulent world of professional football.

The 1970s marked a turning point, a cinematic touchdown if you will, with films like "North Dallas Forty" (1979) pulling back the curtain on the grit and glamour of professional football. This era ushered in a new wave of storytelling, showcasing the sport not merely as a spectacle but as a canvas upon which tales of ambition, camaraderie, and sacrifice could be painted. Nick Nolte's breakthrough performance in "North Dallas Forty" epitomized the shift towards nuanced character portrayals, laying the groundwork for future films to explore the darker, more complex facets of the game.

"Brian's Song" (1971) brought tears to the eyes of audiences, not just for its poignant portrayal of friendship and tragedy but for its groundbreaking depiction of black athletes in the NFL. As cinema increasingly became a mirror reflecting societal changes, football movies emerged as a powerful vehicle for social commentary, challenging stereotypes and pushing the boundaries of representation.

The 1990s and early 2000s witnessed a cinematic blitzkrieg, with films like "Rudy" (1993) and "Any Given Sunday" (1999) taking center stage. These films delved into the underdog narrative and the brutal realities of professional football, transcending the field to explore universal themes of perseverance and the cost of chasing dreams. "Rudy" in particular, with Sean Astin's breakout performance, transformed a simple sports story into a timeless parable of tenacity.

The turn of the millennium brought forth films like "The Replacements" (2000) and "The Blind Side" (2009), each offering a unique perspective on the game. While the former capitalized on the chaos of the 1987 Players' Strike for comedic effect, the latter presented a heartwarming true story with Sandra Bullock's Oscar-winning performance, all the while addressing racial and economic issues beneath its uplifting narrative.

As we delve into the mid-2000s with "Invincible" (2006) and "Jerry Maguire" (1996), the narrative lens widens to encompass not just the players on the field but the impact of their stories on a broader cultural landscape. Mark Wahlberg's portrayal of Vince Papale in "Invincible" anchored a Disney sports drama that reinforced the enduring appeal of the underdog narrative, while "Jerry Maguire" birthed a catchphrase that transcended its cinematic origins, echoing through the corridors of popular culture.

"Draft Day" (2014) serves as a cinematic bookend, pulling back the curtain on the high-stakes drama of the NFL Draft. In doing so, it invites audiences to ponder not just the intricacies of the draft process but the larger-than-life narratives that unfold behind the scenes, blurring the lines between fiction and reality.

Throughout this cinematic odyssey, football has emerged as more than just a sport—it's a prism through which filmmakers refract the complexities of the human experience. Each film in our exploration not only tells a story about football but also becomes a narrative vessel for exploring themes of identity, adversity, triumph, and societal change. As we navigate the reel world of the NFL, we invite you to join us in dissecting the evolution of football's presence on the silver screen, where every frame holds a story as captivating as the last.

## Choosing the 10 Most Iconic Films About the NFL

As we step into the vast arena of NFL cinema, the task at hand is as formidable as a goal-line stand in the dying seconds of the Super Bowl: selecting the 10 most iconic films about the National Football League. This cinematic lineup is more than a mere list; it's a curated collection of narratives that have left an indelible mark on both the realms of football and cinema. Crafting this selection involves a delicate dance between box office success, critical acclaim, cultural impact, and the enduring resonance of the stories told on the silver screen.

The challenge lies not only in identifying films that encapsulate the spirit of the NFL but also in acknowledging the diverse narratives that have shaped the perception of this beloved sport. From classic underdog tales to gritty exposés of the game's darker sides, each film chosen for this elite roster offers a unique lens through which we can peer into the heart of football culture.

Our journey begins with "The Longest Yard" (1974), a film that not only set the tone for the gridiron genre but also established the precedent for the intersection of football and rebellion. The selection of this film is not just based on its commercial success or Burt Reynolds' charismatic turn; it is a nod to the way it laid the groundwork for a cinematic exploration of football as a microcosm of societal dynamics.

Moving forward in time but not in intensity, "North Dallas Forty" (1979) secures its place in the pantheon of NFL films by pulling back the curtain on the glamour and grit behind professional football. Nick Nolte's breakthrough role in this film is more than just a performance; it's a milestone in the evolution of football storytelling, revealing the complexities that lie beneath the gladiatorial spectacle on the field.

"Brian's Song" (1971) earns its spot not just for its tearjerking narrative but for the revolutionary way it portrayed the friendship between Gale Sayers and Brian Piccolo. As the NFL grappled with issues of race and identity, this film became a cinematic touchstone, challenging stereotypes and offering a new perspective on the experiences of black athletes in the league.

The selection of "Rudy" (1993) on our list goes beyond the feel-good underdog story. It delves into the very essence of sports storytelling, where the triumph of the human spirit takes center stage. Sean Astin's portrayal of Rudy Ruettiger catapults this film into the echelons of NFL cinema, not merely as a sports drama but as a testament to the enduring allure of the ultimate underdog tale.

"The Replacements" (2000) earns its position by embracing the chaos of the 1987 Players' Strike and fashioning it into a comedic narrative that dances on the fringes of reality. Keanu Reeves leads a ragtag team of replacement players, delivering a film that, despite its need for suspension of disbelief, captures the essence of camaraderie and the enduring appeal of football even in the face of disruption.

Oliver Stone's "Any Given Sunday" (1999) storms onto our list with its hyperkinetic football epic, where Al Pacino commands as a beleaguered coach navigating the brutal terrain of professional football. Stone's theatrical flourishes and unflinching portrayal of the sport's darker side elevate this film beyond mere sports drama, marking a point of departure in the cinematic exploration of football's underbelly.

"The Blind Side" (2009) secures its spot not just for Sandra Bullock's Oscar-winning performance but for its exploration of racial and economic issues simmering beneath the uplifting tale of Michael Oher. This film becomes a cultural touchstone, using football as a lens to examine societal structures and challenges.

"Invincible" (2006) claims its position by anchoring the improbable NFL dream of Vince Papale in the heart of Philadelphia. Mark Wahlberg's portrayal, combined with the lean and formulaic retelling of a real-life miracle season, positions this film as a quintessential Disney sports drama that contributes to the enduring lore of underdog triumphs.

"Jerry Maguire" (1996) makes the cut not just for the iconic catchphrase "Show me the money" but for Tom Cruise's charismatic portrayal of a sports agent navigating the cutthroat world of professional football. The film's dramedy balance earns it widespread appeal, and its lasting cultural impact extends far beyond the realm of sports cinema.

"Draft Day" (2014) closes our list, pulling back the curtain on the NFL Draft and weaving a character study rather than a hard-hitting drama. Kevin Costner leads an ensemble cast in a film that piggybacks on the intrigue of the real draft, inviting audiences to witness the high-stakes machinations behind the scenes of professional football.

These 10 films, each meticulously chosen, represent not only a journey through the cinematic landscapes of football but also a testament to the enduring power of storytelling. As we delve into the analysis of each film in the chapters that follow, we invite you to join us in exploring the nuances, the triumphs, and the challenges woven into the fabric of these iconic NFL movies.

## Themes and Comparisons to Be Explored

As we embark on a cinematic journey through the annals of NFL films, the stories we encounter transcend the boundaries of the gridiron, weaving a tapestry of narratives that resonate far beyond the confines of the playing field. Within this vast landscape of football storytelling, common threads and recurring motifs emerge, inviting us to explore the nuanced themes that bind these diverse narratives together. In this chapter, we delve into the thematic undercurrents that course through the veins of our chosen 10 iconic NFL films, unraveling the complexities, triumphs, and challenges that define the relationship between football and cinema.

The Struggle for Identity and Belonging: One of the unifying themes across these films is the exploration of characters grappling with their identity and seeking a sense of belonging. From the inmates in "The Longest Yard" (1974) finding camaraderie on the makeshift football field to Rudy Ruettiger's relentless pursuit of acceptance in "Rudy" (1993), the gridiron becomes a proving ground for characters striving to define themselves in the face of societal expectations and personal limitations. This theme is not confined to the players alone; coaches, agents, and even the fans navigate their own paths of self-discovery against the backdrop of the football world.

The Underdog Narrative: The underdog narrative stands as a pillar in the foundation of NFL cinema, and our selection of films reflects this enduring appeal. "Rudy" (1993), "Invincible" (2006), and "The Replacements" (2000) all center around protagonists defying the odds, embodying the collective spirit of the ultimate comeback. Whether it's a walk-on player dreaming of making the team, an everyday guy with dreams of playing in the NFL, or a group of replacement players seeking redemption, these narratives reinforce the timeless allure of triumph against adversity.

The Complexities of Leadership: Leadership, in its myriad forms, emerges as a recurring theme across our selection of films. From coaches navigating the tumultuous world of professional football in "Any Given Sunday" (1999) and "Draft Day" (2014) to the ragtag team of replacements finding an unexpected leader in "The Replacements" (2000), the films dissect the dynamics of leadership within the context of the sport. These narratives showcase the burdens, responsibilities, and transformative power that come with leading a team, whether on the field or from the front office.

Race Relations and Social Dynamics: The evolution of race relations and social dynamics within the context of the NFL serves as a rich vein for exploration in our chosen films. "Brian's Song" (1971) stands as a poignant example, breaking barriers with its portrayal of the friendship between Gale Sayers and Brian Piccolo. "The Blind Side" (2009) and "Remember the Titans" (2000) extend this exploration, delving into racial and socioeconomic issues that simmer beneath the surface of the game. The films offer a lens through which to examine the broader social landscape, highlighting both progress and persisting challenges.

Commercialization and Culture: As the NFL transformed into a cultural juggernaut, the intersection of commercialization and the intrinsic values of the sport became a subject of exploration in our cinematic lineup. "Jerry Maguire" (1996) invites viewers into the cutthroat world of sports agents, where the pursuit of profit intersects with the passion for the game. Similarly, "Any Given Sunday" (1999) peels back the layers of glamour to reveal the commodification of players and the impact of a hyper-commercialized league on the sport's core values. These films question the delicate balance between the business of football and its cultural significance.

Football as an Allegory for Life's Lessons: Beyond the touchdowns and tackles, our selection of films positions football as a metaphor for life itself. "The Longest Yard" (1974) and "Any Given Sunday" (1999) expose the brutal realities of existence, portraying the game as a microcosm of the struggles, triumphs, and moral dilemmas faced by individuals in society. These films offer audiences a mirror to reflect on their own journeys, using the gridiron as a stage for the larger drama of life.

Critiques of Heroism and Myth-Making: The construction of heroes and the mythology surrounding football legends form a critical backdrop in our exploration. "Rudy" (1993) questions the truth behind the legend, inviting audiences to ponder the fine line between inspiration and embellishment. "Invincible" (2006) and "Jerry Maguire" (1996) similarly dissect the hero narrative, exposing the vulnerabilities and human dimensions that often lie beneath the veneer of greatness. These films challenge the traditional notions of heroism and compel viewers to question the narratives they hold dear.

New Styles and Perspectives in Sports Films: As the cinematic landscape evolves, so too do the styles and perspectives employed in the portrayal of sports on screen. "The Blind Side" (2009) and "Draft Day" (2014) exemplify this evolution, employing innovative storytelling techniques and character studies that transcend the traditional sports drama formula. These films mark a departure from conventional narratives, embracing new styles that reflect the changing tastes of audiences and the dynamic nature of cinematic storytelling.

As we traverse the thematic landscapes of these iconic NFL films, we invite you to join us in unraveling the layers of meaning, dissecting the intricacies, and exploring the profound reflections of the human experience that lie within each frame. In the chapters that follow, we delve deep into the narratives, characters, and themes that make these films not just stories about football but timeless reflections of the human condition.

## Chapter 1: The Longest Yard (1974)
## The Inspiration: Movies Set in Prison

In the hallowed halls of cinematic history, few films have managed to meld the harsh realities of prison life with the gritty spectacle of professional football as seamlessly as "The Longest Yard" (1974). Before we delve into the gridiron battles and the clash of titans on the field, it's imperative to understand the unique blend of inspiration that fueled the creation of this iconic film. The genesis of "The Longest Yard" owes much to the rich tapestry of movies set in prison, a genre that, at its core, explores the depths of the human spirit within the confines of incarceration.

The prison film genre has long been a canvas for storytellers to depict the struggle for survival, the quest for redemption, and the indomitable nature of the human spirit under the oppressive weight of confinement. It's within this genre that "The Longest Yard" finds its roots, drawing upon the thematic elements and narrative tropes that have come to define prison cinema.

From Chain Gangs to Gridirons: A Cinematic Evolution: The history of movies set in prison is a storied one, tracing its origins to the early days of cinema with classics like "The Big House" (1930) and "I Am a Fugitive from a Chain Gang" (1932). These early films laid the foundation for exploring the dehumanizing aspects of prison life, portraying characters ensnared in a web of brutality, injustice, and the quest for freedom.

As the years progressed, the prison genre evolved, adopting new tones and perspectives. Films like "Cool Hand Luke" (1967) brought a sense of rebelliousness and anti-authoritarianism to the genre, featuring charismatic protagonists who resisted the dehumanizing effects of imprisonment. This rebellious spirit would later find a home in "The Longest Yard," where the gridiron becomes both a battleground for physical prowess and a symbolic arena for resistance against authority.

The Longest Yard's Unique Blend: Released in 1974, "The Longest Yard" arrived at a juncture where the prison film genre had matured, and its tropes were ripe for reinterpretation. Enter Burt Reynolds as Paul Crewe, a disgraced former professional football player who finds himself incarcerated. What sets "The Longest Yard" apart is its audacious fusion of the prison drama with the testosterone-fueled spectacle of football. Director Robert Aldrich and screenwriter Tracy Keenan Wynn took inspiration from the conventions of prison films, infusing them with the adrenaline-pumping energy of the gridiron.

In the film, the prison setting becomes a microcosm of society, complete with power struggles, alliances, and a pervasive sense of injustice. Paul Crewe, initially a cynical and self-centered individual, transforms within the confines of the prison walls, echoing the character arcs seen in classic prison dramas. His journey mirrors that of protagonists in films like "The Shawshank Redemption" (1994), where imprisonment becomes a crucible for personal redemption and the forging of unexpected alliances.

Gridiron as Battleground: The marriage of prison and football in "The Longest Yard" is more than a narrative gimmick; it's a stroke of genius that elevates the film to a unique position within both genres. The football sequences within the prison setting bring a visceral intensity to the screen, with bone-crushing tackles and hard-hitting action mirroring the brutality of life behind bars. The gridiron becomes a metaphorical battleground where the struggles of the characters transcend the physical contest, encapsulating themes of resistance, camaraderie, and the pursuit of dignity.

In many ways, the football sequences in "The Longest Yard" pay homage to the physicality and resilience often associated with prison life. The players, many of whom are fellow inmates, channel their frustrations and desires for retribution into the game, blurring the lines between sport and survival. The film taps into the archetype of the underdog, a motif that resonates deeply within both the prison and sports genres, as characters defy expectations and societal norms.

Influence on Later Prison Films: "The Longest Yard" not only drew inspiration from the prison film genre but also left an indelible mark, influencing subsequent films that explored the intersection of sports and incarceration. The film's success paved the way for a subgenre where sports became the vehicle for both personal redemption and societal critique within the prison context.

Movies like "Mean Machine" (2001), a British adaptation with soccer as the sport of choice, and the 2005 remake of "The Longest Yard" itself, starring Adam Sandler, continued the tradition of blending sports drama with the dynamics of life behind bars. These films, in their own ways, paid homage to the thematic groundwork laid by "The Longest Yard," proving the enduring appeal of exploring the human spirit in the crucible of both sports and incarceration.

Conclusion: The Legacy of The Longest Yard's Prison Roots: As we unravel the layers of "The Longest Yard," it becomes evident that the film's roots in the prison genre contribute to its enduring legacy. The unique synthesis of prison drama and football spectacle creates a narrative alchemy that transcends the constraints of genre conventions. The film stands as a testament to the malleability of cinematic genres, demonstrating that, when done with finesse, disparate elements can coalesce into a compelling and resonant narrative.

"The Longest Yard" not only pays homage to the rich history of prison films but also reshapes and revitalizes the genre by injecting it with the pulse-pounding energy of sports drama. As we delve deeper into the chapters that follow, the influence of the prison genre on "The Longest Yard" will continue to reverberate, providing a thematic foundation for the exploration of football, rebellion, and the triumph of the human spirit on the silver screen.

## Burt Reynolds Cements His Star Status

In the hallowed halls of Hollywood, there are moments when an actor transcends mere stardom to become an iconic figure, forever etched in the annals of cinematic history. For Burt Reynolds, "The Longest Yard" (1974) stands as a defining chapter in his career—a film that not only showcased his undeniable charisma and rugged charm but also catapulted him into the pantheon of leading men in the 1970s. As we explore the impact of "The Longest Yard" and its intersection with Burt Reynolds's career, we uncover a narrative of talent, timing, and the transformation of an actor into a bona fide star.

Burt Reynolds: The Journey to The Longest Yard: Before he donned the prison stripes of Paul Crewe, Burt Reynolds had already carved a niche for himself in Hollywood. Emerging from a background in television and smaller film roles, Reynolds's journey to leading man status was marked by perseverance, versatility, and a rugged charm that set him apart. Films like "Deliverance" (1972) and "White Lightning" (1973) showcased his dramatic range and established him as a bankable actor. However, it was "The Longest Yard" that would not only define his career trajectory but also solidify his status as a Hollywood leading man.

Reynolds's casting as Paul Crewe was serendipitous in many ways. The role required a balance of charisma, athleticism, and a roguish charm—a combination that Reynolds effortlessly brought to the table. His magnetic screen presence, coupled with a natural athleticism derived from his collegiate football background, made him the ideal choice to portray a fallen football star navigating the brutal confines of a prison setting.

The Charisma of Paul Crewe: In "The Longest Yard," Reynolds inhabited the character of Paul Crewe with a magnetic charisma that resonated with audiences. Crewe, a former professional quarterback turned disgraced convict, is a complex figure, a blend of cocky arrogance and an underlying vulnerability that Reynolds navigates with a nuanced touch. As the narrative unfolds, Reynolds infuses Crewe with a sense of roguish charm, endearing him to viewers even as he grapples with the consequences of his actions.

It's this charisma that serves as the linchpin of the film's success. Reynolds's ability to embody the antihero with a twinkle in his eye—the man who's both a rebel and a reluctant leader—creates a character that transcends the confines of the genre. Whether orchestrating plays on the football field or navigating the power dynamics within the prison walls, Reynolds as Crewe becomes a symbol of resilience, rebellion, and, ultimately, redemption.

The Physicality of the Role: In portraying Paul Crewe, Reynolds not only had to convey emotional depth but also had to embody the physical prowess expected of a former professional athlete. The football sequences within the film demanded more than just acting; they required a level of athleticism that few actors could muster. Reynolds, with his background as a college football player, brought an authenticity to the role that resonated with audiences and added credibility to the on-screen gridiron battles.

The film's success hinged on the believability of Reynolds as a quarterback, and his commitment to the physicality of the role elevated "The Longest Yard" beyond a mere sports drama. The raw energy he brought to the football scenes, whether throwing a touchdown pass or taking a hard hit, mirrored the visceral intensity of the sport itself. Reynolds's dedication to the physical demands of the role showcased his commitment to authenticity and added a layer of realism to the film's depiction of football within the prison setting.

A Star Turn that Transcends Genre: While "The Longest Yard" is undeniably a sports film, Reynolds's performance ensured that it transcended the boundaries of genre. His portrayal of Paul Crewe not only anchored the film but also transformed it into a character-driven narrative with universal appeal. Reynolds's ability to inject humor, vulnerability, and a rebellious spirit into the character resonated with audiences, making Crewe more than just a fallen athlete—he became an emblem of defiance in the face of adversity.

The film's success at the box office and with critics was, in no small part, a testament to Reynolds's star power. He took what could have been a straightforward sports drama and infused it with a personality that went beyond the confines of the genre. Reynolds's charm and charisma turned Paul Crewe into an iconic character, and in doing so, he elevated himself to the status of a leading man who could carry a film with both swagger and substance.

Impact on Reynolds's Career Trajectory: "The Longest Yard" was a turning point for Burt Reynolds, both in terms of recognition and the types of roles he would subsequently undertake. The film's success not only solidified his position as a bankable leading man but also opened doors to a diverse range of projects. Reynolds's newfound status as a Hollywood star allowed him to explore different genres, from action films like "Smokey and the Bandit" (1977) to comedies like "The Cannonball Run" (1981), showcasing the versatility that would define his career.

Reynolds's ability to balance tough-guy roles with comedic flair mirrored the complex persona he introduced in "The Longest Yard." The film marked the beginning of a prolific period for Reynolds, where he would become one of the most bankable stars of the 1970s and '80s. The impact of "The Longest Yard" reverberated not only in the success of the film itself but in the trajectory of Reynolds's career, positioning him as an enduring icon in the pantheon of Hollywood leading men.

Legacy and Cultural Impact: "The Longest Yard" endures not only as a classic sports film but as a testament to the charisma and star power of Burt Reynolds. The character of Paul Crewe remains an indelible part of cinematic history, and Reynolds's portrayal of the rebellious quarterback turned reluctant leader has left an enduring imprint on popular culture.

Reynolds's star status, cemented by his performance in "The Longest Yard," transcended the confines of the film, shaping the narrative of his career for years to come. His ability to inject nuance, humor, and authenticity into characters became a hallmark of his subsequent roles, and the film stands as a milestone that marks the ascent of Burt Reynolds to Hollywood royalty.

As we delve deeper into "The Longest Yard," the intersection of Burt Reynolds's star power with the rebellious spirit of Paul Crewe becomes a focal point for understanding the film's enduring appeal. Reynolds's journey from a promising actor to a Hollywood icon finds its zenith in "The Longest Yard," where the charisma of the man and the character become inseparable, creating a cinematic alchemy that continues to captivate audiences and define an era of Hollywood stardom.

**Critically Acclaimed, Commercially Successful**

In the tumultuous landscape of Hollywood, where critical acclaim and box office success often occupy opposing ends of the spectrum, "The Longest Yard" (1974) emerges as a rare intersection—a film that not only resonated with audiences but also garnered praise from critics. As we dissect the critical and commercial dimensions of this iconic sports drama, we uncover the delicate balance struck by director Robert Aldrich, screenwriter Tracy Keenan Wynn, and the ensemble cast led by Burt Reynolds. The critical acclaim bestowed upon the film not only validated its artistic merits but also contributed to its enduring legacy as a cinematic classic.

Critical Acclaim: Crafting a Sports Drama with Depth: "The Longest Yard" arrived at a juncture where the sports film genre was evolving. No longer confined to formulaic underdog narratives, audiences and critics alike were beginning to appreciate films that transcended the boundaries of their genres, offering nuanced storytelling and complex characters. In this landscape, "The Longest Yard" stood out as a film that not only delivered thrilling football sequences but also delved into the human drama within the prison walls.

Character Depth and Nuanced Storytelling: At the heart of the critical acclaim was the film's ability to infuse depth into its characters, elevating them beyond mere sports archetypes. Paul Crewe, portrayed by Burt Reynolds, wasn't just a fallen football star; he was a complex figure navigating the complexities of pride, redemption, and reluctant leadership. The film's ensemble cast, including Eddie Albert as the warden and James Hampton as Caretaker, brought a richness to their characters that resonated with critics. The dynamics between the inmates, the prison staff, and the football team added layers to the narrative, transforming "The Longest Yard" into a character-driven drama with universal themes.

Subversion of Sports Movie Tropes: One aspect that garnered critical acclaim was the film's subversion of traditional sports movie tropes. Instead of a straightforward underdog tale, "The Longest Yard" introduced shades of moral ambiguity, rebellion, and the exploration of power dynamics within the prison setting. The decision to set a football film within the confines of a prison added layers of complexity to the narrative, challenging expectations and offering a fresh perspective on both sports and incarceration.

Nuanced Exploration of Themes: The film's exploration of themes such as resilience, redemption, and the clash between authority and rebellion resonated with critics. "The Longest Yard" wasn't merely a sports movie; it was a social commentary wrapped in the guise of a football drama. The nuanced exploration of societal issues within the microcosm of a prison setting elevated the film beyond the gridiron, earning praise for its ability to tackle weighty themes without sacrificing the entertainment value.

Burt Reynolds: A Star Turn that Transcends Sports: Central to the critical success of "The Longest Yard" was the star-making performance of Burt Reynolds. Critics lauded Reynolds not only for his athletic prowess on the field but for the depth and charisma he brought to the character of Paul

Crewe. Reynolds's ability to navigate the complexities of an antihero—a fallen football star with a rebellious streak—was a revelation, showcasing a dimension of his talent that extended beyond the tough-guy roles he had previously portrayed.

Charismatic and Multifaceted Performance: Reynolds infused Paul Crewe with a magnetic charisma that became the heartbeat of the film. His roguish charm and undeniable screen presence transformed Crewe from a sports archetype into a fully realized character. Critics celebrated Reynolds's performance for its multifaceted nature—he could be humorous and vulnerable in one moment and commanding and rebellious in the next. The actor's ability to convey the internal conflicts of Crewe added layers to the film, earning him accolades for a performance that transcended the expectations of a traditional sports movie.

Chemistry with the Ensemble Cast: The chemistry between Reynolds and the ensemble cast further contributed to the critical success of the film. The camaraderie between the inmates, the tension with the prison staff, and the dynamics within the football team felt authentic, thanks to the synergy among the actors. Critics highlighted the ensemble's ability to bring their characters to life, creating a believable and immersive world within the confines of the prison.

Balancing Humor and Drama: "The Longest Yard" showcased Reynolds's versatility as an actor, seamlessly balancing humor and drama. The film's comedic elements, often arising from the interactions between the inmates, added levity to the narrative without diminishing its emotional impact. Reynolds's comedic timing and ability to infuse humor into the character of Crewe endeared him to both critics and audiences, solidifying his status as a leading man capable of navigating the nuanced terrain of sports dramedy.

Box Office Triumph: The Mass Appeal of Football and Rebellion: While critical acclaim laid the foundation for "The Longest Yard's" enduring legacy, its commercial success catapulted it into the realm of box office triumph. The film's ability to resonate with a broad audience, tapping into the universal appeal of football and the themes of rebellion and triumph, contributed to its widespread popularity.

Appealing to Sports Enthusiasts: Football, with its status as America's favorite sport, has always had a special place in the hearts of audiences. "The Longest Yard" capitalized on this inherent appeal, offering thrilling gridiron action that rivaled the excitement of a real NFL game. The film's football sequences, choreographed with a visceral intensity, drew sports enthusiasts to theaters, eager to witness a cinematic portrayal of the game they loved.

Transcending Sports: What set "The Longest Yard" apart was its ability to transcend the sports movie niche. While it delivered on the expectations of football enthusiasts with its dynamic and well-executed game sequences, the film's broader themes of rebellion, camaraderie, and redemption appealed to a wider audience. The universal nature of these themes allowed the film to resonate beyond the confines of sports fandom, drawing in viewers who might not typically gravitate toward sports dramas.

Capitalizing on Cultural Dynamics: The early 1970s were marked by a cultural climate of rebellion and questioning authority. "The Longest Yard" tapped into this zeitgeist, presenting a narrative of inmates challenging the establishment within the framework of a football game. The film's depiction of rebellion and defiance struck a chord with audiences who were drawn to the countercultural spirit of the era. This cultural resonance contributed to the film's box office success, as it became more than just a sports movie—it became a reflection of the societal currents of its time.

Enduring Legacy and Continued Reverence: As we revisit "The Longest Yard" through the lens of critical acclaim and commercial success, it becomes evident that the film's legacy is deeply intertwined with its ability to satisfy both the discerning critic and the eager moviegoer. The enduring reverence for the film lies in its capacity to balance the artistry of storytelling with the mass appeal of sports drama.

Impact on Subsequent Sports Films: "The Longest Yard" left an indelible mark on the sports film genre, influencing subsequent films that sought to blend sports spectacle with nuanced storytelling. The success of the film demonstrated that audiences were hungry for sports narratives that went beyond the predictable underdog formula. Filmmakers began to recognize the potential for sports dramas to tackle weighty themes while still delivering the excitement of the game.

Burt Reynolds: A Hollywood Icon: The critical and commercial success of "The Longest Yard" elevated Burt Reynolds to the status of a Hollywood icon. Reynolds's star turn in the film not only solidified his leading man status but also opened doors to a range of roles that showcased his versatility. The film marked a pivotal moment in Reynolds's career, setting the stage for a prolific period that would see him become one of the most recognizable and beloved actors of the era.

Enduring Popularity: "The Longest Yard" continues to enjoy a lasting popularity that transcends generations. Its timeless themes of rebellion, camaraderie, and triumph over adversity ensure its relevance, and the film remains a staple in discussions of both sports cinema and the broader cultural landscape. The enduring popularity of "The Longest Yard" speaks to its ability to resonate with audiences across decades, cementing its place as a classic in the pantheon of American cinema.

As we move forward in our exploration of "The Longest Yard," we carry with us an appreciation for the delicate equilibrium achieved by the film—a balance between critical acclaim and commercial success that has allowed it to endure as a cultural touchstone. In the chapters that follow, we delve deeper into the layers of this cinematic gem, uncovering the intricate details that contribute to its status as a critically acclaimed and commercially successful classic.

## Depictions of Masculinity and Rebellion

In the testosterone-laden arena of professional football, where physical prowess and a rugged demeanor often define masculinity, "The Longest Yard" (1974) emerges as a cinematic exploration of the complexities inherent in the construct of manhood. Beyond the electrifying football sequences and the confines of the prison setting, the film delves into the nuanced depictions of masculinity, rebellion, and the challenges of asserting individuality within a system defined by authority. As we dissect these thematic layers, we uncover a narrative that transcends the gridiron, offering a compelling commentary on the intersections of masculinity and rebellion.

Masculinity on the Gridiron: At the heart of "The Longest Yard" lies the juxtaposition of masculinity and vulnerability, embodied by the film's central character, Paul Crewe, played by Burt Reynolds. The world of professional football has long been associated with traditional notions of masculinity—strength, toughness, and a certain stoicism in the face of physical adversity. Crewe, once a celebrated quarterback, finds himself navigating a new definition of masculinity within the confines of a prison.

Physicality and Athleticism: The film's portrayal of masculinity on the football field is a visceral spectacle, capturing the essence of the sport in bone-crushing tackles, powerful throws, and strategic plays. The inmates, predominantly male, channel their physical prowess into the game, showcasing a form of masculinity that transcends the limitations of their incarcerated existence. The football sequences become a battleground where traditional markers of manhood—physical strength, agility, and competitiveness—are amplified.

Vulnerability and Redemption: However, the film goes beyond the physicality of the sport to explore the vulnerability and redemption of its central character. Paul Crewe, initially presented as a cocky and self-centered figure, undergoes a transformation that challenges conventional notions of masculinity. His journey—from fallen football star to reluctant leader—introduces vulnerability into the narrative, disrupting the rigid expectations associated with traditional masculinity.

Crewe's vulnerability is not limited to his physical struggles on the field but extends to his emotional and psychological battles. The film deftly explores the impact of societal expectations on the construction of masculinity, portraying Crewe's internal conflicts and the quest for redemption as integral components of his journey toward self-discovery.

Rebellion as a Form of Defiance: Central to the narrative of "The Longest Yard" is the theme of rebellion—a defiant stance against authority and a refusal to conform to the expectations imposed by the prison system. The characters, predominantly male inmates, navigate a world where rebellion becomes a survival mechanism, a means of asserting agency within the confines of a rigid structure.

Football as a Vehicle for Rebellion: The choice to set the rebellion within the framework of a football game is a masterstroke, as it merges the physicality of the sport with the inmates' desire to defy authority. The football field becomes a symbolic battleground where the inmates, led by Crewe, rebel against the oppressive regime of the prison warden. The act of organizing and participating in the game becomes an assertion of autonomy, a collective rebellion that transcends the boundaries of the gridiron.

Defying Stereotypes: "The Longest Yard" challenges stereotypes associated with masculinity by presenting a diverse array of male characters within the prison setting. While some conform to traditional expectations of toughness and aggression, others subvert these stereotypes, displaying vulnerability, intelligence, and a capacity for empathy. The film portrays rebellion not as a monolithic expression of masculinity but as a multifaceted endeavor shaped by individual circumstances and motivations.

Individualism in Rebellion: The inmates, each with their own reasons for rebelling, contribute to a collective narrative that celebrates individualism within the broader theme of defiance. The rebellion is not a homogenous expression but a mosaic of personal struggles against injustice, abuse, and the dehumanizing aspects of the prison system. This individualism within rebellion reinforces the idea that masculinity, like the inmates themselves, is not a monolithic concept but a spectrum of identities shaped by personal experiences.

Authority and the Struggle for Autonomy: The struggle against authority in "The Longest Yard" is not merely a physical battle on the football field but a deeper exploration of the inmates' quest for autonomy within a system designed to strip them of their individuality. The prison warden, epitomizing institutional authority, becomes the embodiment of a system that seeks to suppress the autonomy and agency of the incarcerated men.

Warden Hazen: The Face of Authority: Warden Hazen, portrayed by Eddie Albert, symbolizes the authoritarian figurehead within the narrative. His control over the inmates extends beyond the physical confines of the prison, reaching into the very fabric of their lives. The warden's determination to assert dominance and maintain control becomes a catalyst for the inmates' rebellion, transforming the football game into an arena where the struggle for autonomy plays out in a visceral manner.

Football as a Metaphor for Autonomy: The act of organizing and participating in the football game becomes a metaphor for autonomy—a brief respite from the dehumanizing routines of prison life. The inmates, through their rebellion on the field, reclaim a sense of agency and self-determination. The game becomes a fleeting moment where they can assert their humanity, challenge the authority of the warden, and experience a taste of freedom within the confines of their incarceration.

The Power Dynamics of Rebellion: "The Longest Yard" carefully navigates the power dynamics inherent in the struggle for autonomy. The inmates, while rebelling against the authority of the warden, also grapple with internal power struggles within their own ranks. The dynamics between Crewe and the other inmates, particularly Caretaker (James

Hampton), add layers to the narrative, illustrating the complexities of asserting autonomy within a community bound by shared confinement.

Navigating Themes of Masculinity and Rebellion: As "The Longest Yard" navigates the themes of masculinity and rebellion, it transcends the conventional sports movie formula, offering a nuanced exploration of identity, vulnerability, and the complexities of resistance within a system designed to strip away individuality. The film's ability to infuse traditional markers of masculinity with vulnerability, and rebellion with a quest for autonomy, elevates it into a realm of cinematic storytelling that resonates far beyond the football field and prison walls.

Breaking the Mold of Sports Cinema: The film's approach to masculinity challenges the established norms of sports cinema, which often emphasizes physical prowess and stoic heroism. By introducing vulnerability and internal conflicts into the narrative, "The Longest Yard" defies the conventional expectations associated with sports movies. The exploration of rebellion as a multifaceted endeavor further breaks the mold, presenting a collective act of defiance that is as diverse as the individuals involved.

Individualism within Collective Rebellion: "The Longest Yard" celebrates individualism within the context of collective rebellion, emphasizing that the quest for autonomy is deeply personal and shaped by individual circumstances. Each inmate, with his unique background and motivations, contributes to the rebellion in his own way. The film invites viewers to empathize with the diverse experiences of the characters, showcasing that masculinity is not a monolithic construct but a spectrum of identities shaped by personal struggles and aspirations.

Autonomy as a Fleeting Victory: The film's portrayal of autonomy as a fleeting victory within the football game echoes the broader societal struggles against systemic oppression. While the inmates experience a brief respite on the field, the reality of their incarceration looms large. This dichotomy reinforces the film's exploration of rebellion as a complex and ongoing endeavor—one that acknowledges the challenges of asserting autonomy within a system designed to maintain control.

Legacy and Continued Relevance: As we dissect the depictions of masculinity and rebellion in "The Longest Yard," it becomes clear that the film's thematic richness has contributed to its enduring legacy. Beyond the visceral excitement of football sequences and the rebellion against authority, the narrative offers a profound exploration of the human experience within the intersection of masculinity and resistance.

Influence on Subsequent Narratives: "The Longest Yard" has left an indelible mark on subsequent narratives that explore masculinity, rebellion, and the complexities of identity. The film's approach to subverting traditional sports movie tropes has influenced filmmakers to delve deeper into the psychological and emotional dimensions of sports narratives. Themes of vulnerability and rebellion, once considered unconventional in sports cinema, have become integral to contemporary narratives that seek to challenge and expand the genre.

Relevance in Societal Discourse: The film's exploration of rebellion and the struggle for autonomy remains relevant in broader societal discourse. The themes resonate with discussions around systemic oppression, institutional control, and the ongoing quest for individual agency. "The Longest Yard" serves as a cinematic touchstone that invites audiences to reflect on the intersections of masculinity and rebellion within the context of larger societal structures.

Legacy of Burt Reynolds's Performance: Burt Reynolds's portrayal of Paul Crewe, with its nuanced depiction of vulnerability and rebellion, has become a benchmark for actors navigating complex male characters. Reynolds's performance in "The Longest Yard" not only contributed to the film's critical acclaim but also established him as an actor capable of infusing traditional masculine archetypes with depth and authenticity. The legacy of Reynolds's performance extends beyond the film, influencing subsequent portrayals of masculinity in cinema.

Conclusion: Unraveling Layers of Masculinity and Rebellion: As we conclude our exploration of "The Longest Yard's" depictions of masculinity and rebellion, we unravel the layers of complexity that define the film's narrative. The fusion of traditional markers of masculinity with vulnerability, and the exploration of rebellion as a multifaceted endeavor, elevate the film into a realm of cinematic storytelling that transcends genre conventions.

"The Longest Yard" invites audiences to engage with themes that resonate far beyond the football field—a reflection on the constructs of masculinity, the dynamics of rebellion, and the enduring quest for autonomy within systems of power. The film's ability to navigate these themes with nuance and authenticity contributes to its lasting legacy, ensuring that, decades after its release, it remains a poignant and relevant exploration of the human spirit within the confines of both sports and incarceration.

## Chapter 2: North Dallas Forty (1979)
## Pulling Back the Curtain on Pro Football

In the shadow of the glitzy and often idealized portrayal of professional football on the silver screen, "North Dallas Forty" (1979) emerges as a gritty and unflinching exposé, pulling back the curtain on the behind-the-scenes reality of the sport. Directed by Ted Kotcheff and based on the semi-autobiographical novel by Peter Gent, the film offers a stark departure from the heroic narratives often associated with football movies. As we delve into the narrative layers of "North Dallas Forty," we unravel a compelling exploration of the complexities, contradictions, and harsh realities that define the professional football landscape.

The Illusion of Glory: "North Dallas Forty" opens with a poignant statement—football is not a contact sport; it's a collision sport. This declaration sets the tone for a film that challenges the romanticized notions of glory, camaraderie, and heroism often attributed to professional football. The movie, set in the world of the North Dallas Bulls, a fictionalized version of the Dallas Cowboys, shatters the illusion of the pristine and glamorous image associated with America's favorite sport.

Physical Toll on Players: At the heart of pulling back the curtain on pro football is the unapologetic portrayal of the physical toll exacted on players. The film, set against the backdrop of the brutal demands of the sport, delves into the injuries, painkillers, and sheer physical brutality that define the daily lives of professional athletes. The camera doesn't shy away from depicting the aftermath of bone-crushing tackles, the toll of multiple surgeries, and the pervasive use of pain medication—a stark departure from the sanitized image presented on the field.

The Myth of Camaraderie: While the camaraderie of the locker room is a staple of sports films, "North Dallas Forty" exposes the fragility of these relationships in the cutthroat world of professional football. The bonds forged in the locker room are often strained by the pressures of competition, personal ambition, and the transient nature of a player's career. The film presents a nuanced exploration of the camaraderie myth, revealing the tensions that simmer beneath the surface, eroding the idealized image of the tight-knit team.

The Business of Football: As the film peels back the layers of the football world, it unveils the cutthroat business that underpins the sport. "North Dallas Forty" offers a scathing critique of the commodification of athletes and the dehumanizing nature of a system that values performance over well-being.

Player as a Commodity: In the world of professional football, players are commodities—assets to be managed, traded, and discarded based on their perceived value to the team. The film portrays the dehumanizing effects of this commodification, where players are treated as expendable resources, their bodies pushed to the limits for the sake of victory, and their worth measured solely in terms of on-field performance.

Contractual Pressures: The contractual pressures faced by players become a central theme, highlighting the precarious nature of their professional lives. The looming threat of being cut from the team, the pressure to conform to team management's expectations, and the lack of job security create an environment where players are forced to navigate a delicate balance between expressing individuality and conforming to the team's demands.

Nick Nolte's Breakthrough Role: Central to the film's narrative is the powerhouse performance by Nick Nolte in the role of Phil Elliott, a veteran wide receiver navigating the treacherous terrain of professional football. Nolte's portrayal becomes a lens through which the audience witnesses the internal and external struggles faced by athletes in a sport that demands physical sacrifice and unwavering conformity.

Phil Elliott's Internal Struggles: Nolte's Phil Elliott is not the archetypal sports hero. Instead, he is a multifaceted character wrestling with inner demons, including painkiller addiction, existential questions about the meaning of his career, and the constant pressure to conform to the expectations of team management. Nolte's portrayal humanizes the athlete, inviting empathy for the internal conflicts that often remain hidden beneath the veneer of sports stardom.

Confronting Systemic Injustices: Phil Elliott becomes a conduit for the film's broader exploration of systemic injustices within professional football. His defiance against the rigid norms of the sport, including his vocal critique of team management and the league, challenges the status quo. Nolte's nuanced performance brings depth to a character who becomes a symbol of resistance against a system that prioritizes profit over the well-being of its athletes.

Mature Themes Explore Football's Toll: "North Dallas Forty" doesn't shy away from delving into mature themes that explore the toll of professional football on its players, both physically and mentally. The film confronts issues such as substance abuse, the use of painkillers to mask injuries, and the psychological toll of the relentless pursuit of success.

Substance Abuse as Coping Mechanism: One of the film's bold choices is its candid portrayal of substance abuse as a coping mechanism for the physical and emotional pain endured by athletes. The pervasive use of painkillers becomes a poignant commentary on the lengths to which players go to numb themselves to the harsh realities of their profession. "North Dallas Forty" serves as a cinematic mirror, reflecting the broader societal issues tied to substance abuse within the high-stakes world of professional sports.

The Psychological Toll: In addition to the physical toll, the film explores the psychological impact of a career in professional football. The constant pressure to perform, the fear of career-ending injuries, and the existential questions that arise when an athlete confronts the limits of their physical abilities become central themes. "North Dallas Forty" doesn't shy away from the mental health challenges faced by athletes, offering a sobering portrayal of the toll exacted by the sport.

The Lingering Impact on Sports Dramas: "North Dallas Forty" carved a unique space in the landscape of sports dramas, leaving a lasting impact on subsequent films within the genre.

Its unapologetic portrayal of the less glamorous aspects of professional football challenged the conventions of sports cinema and influenced filmmakers to explore the darker and more complex dimensions of athletic careers.

Influence on Subsequent Sports Films: The film's legacy is evident in subsequent sports films that dared to peel back the curtain on the less glamorous aspects of athletic careers. Movies like "Jerry Maguire" (1996), "Any Given Sunday" (1999), and "Concussion" (2015) owe a debt to "North Dallas Forty" for paving the way to more nuanced and realistic depictions of the challenges faced by athletes. The film's influence is seen not only in its thematic exploration but also in its stylistic choices, including handheld camera work that adds a documentary-like authenticity to the storytelling.

Championing Realism Over Idealism: "North Dallas Forty" championed a shift toward realism over idealism in sports dramas. The film's commitment to portraying the harsh realities of professional football set a precedent for filmmakers who sought to move beyond the formulaic triumph-over-adversity narratives. The legacy of "North Dallas Forty" is embedded in its willingness to challenge audience expectations, offering a narrative that embraces the messiness of real-life struggles faced by athletes.

Conclusion: Unveiling the Realities of Pro Football: As we conclude our exploration of "North Dallas Forty," we unveil a cinematic gem that defied conventions to offer an unflinching portrayal of professional football. The film's courage to pull back the curtain on the sport's harsh realities, from the physical toll on players to the cutthroat business of the industry, cements its status as a groundbreaking work in the sports drama genre.

"North Dallas Forty" goes beyond the spectacle of the game, delving into the human cost of pursuing excellence in a sport that often demands more than it gives. Through Nick Nolte's powerhouse performance and the film's uncompromising narrative, we are invited to confront the complexities, contradictions, and systemic injustices that define the world of professional football. In the chapters that follow, we continue our journey through the cinematic landscape of sports, examining films that, like "North Dallas Forty," challenge and reshape our perceptions of the games we hold dear.

## Nick Nolte's Breakthrough Role

In the annals of cinematic history, certain performances transcend the boundaries of a single film, becoming defining moments in an actor's career. Such is the case with Nick Nolte's portrayal of Phil Elliott in "North Dallas Forty" (1979), a performance that not only anchored the film but also marked a watershed moment in Nolte's career. As we delve into the narrative layers of "North Dallas Forty," we unravel the complexities, nuances, and transformative power of Nolte's breakthrough role—a role that not only showcased his formidable acting prowess but also laid the foundation for a prolific and enduring career in Hollywood.

Phil Elliott: A Multifaceted Antihero:

At the heart of "North Dallas Forty" is Phil Elliott, a veteran wide receiver navigating the treacherous landscape of professional football. Nolte's portrayal of Elliott is a departure from the archetypal sports hero—a character defined by his flaws, contradictions, and a profound sense of existential questioning. The decision to cast Nolte in this nuanced role proved to be a masterstroke, as he brought a raw authenticity to a character that defied the conventions of sports cinema.

Navigating the Complexities of Phil Elliott:

Nolte's portrayal of Phil Elliott goes beyond the surface of the sports genre. Elliott is not a one-dimensional hero; he is a complex and conflicted individual grappling with the harsh realities of his profession. Nolte infuses the character with a palpable vulnerability, allowing the audience to empathize with Elliott's internal struggles, both on and off the field. The actor's ability to navigate the complexities of a multifaceted antihero lays the groundwork for a character study that transcends the traditional confines of sports narratives.

Existential Questions and Inner Turmoil:

At the core of Nolte's performance is the exploration of existential questions and inner turmoil that define Phil Elliott. The character's journey becomes a profound examination of identity, purpose, and the toll of a career in professional football. Nolte's portrayal captures the existential angst that arises when an athlete confronts the limits of his physical abilities, the transience of fame, and the cost of conforming to a system that commodifies players.

Defiance Against Convention:

One of the defining aspects of Nolte's breakthrough role is his defiance against the conventions of sports cinema. In an era dominated by heroic portrayals of athletes overcoming adversity, Phil Elliott stands as a symbol of resistance—a character who refuses to conform to the expectations imposed by the genre. Nolte's performance challenges the traditional narrative arc, offering a refreshing departure that elevates "North Dallas Forty" into a realm of cinematic authenticity.

Resistance to Idealized Heroism:

Nolte's portrayal of Phil Elliott resists the idealized heroism often associated with sports dramas. Instead of a triumphant ascent, the character experiences a descent into the harsh realities of his profession. Elliott's refusal to conform to the idealized image of the sports hero becomes a subversive commentary on the commodification of athletes and the toll exacted by a system that prioritizes success over individual well-being. Nolte's commitment to authenticity over idealism becomes a defining characteristic of his breakthrough performance.

Confronting Systemic Injustices:

In addition to defying conventional sports hero tropes, Nolte's portrayal confronts systemic injustices within professional football. Phil Elliott becomes a vessel for expressing discontent with the dehumanizing aspects of the industry—from the pressures of conformity to the commodification of players. Nolte's performance transforms "North Dallas Forty" into a vehicle for social critique, shining a spotlight on the darker corners of the sports world.

Humanizing the Athlete:

Nick Nolte's breakthrough role in "North Dallas Forty" is marked by his ability to humanize the athlete—taking a character that could easily be reduced to a sports archetype and infusing him with layers of humanity, vulnerability, and relatability. This transformative aspect of Nolte's performance reverberates far beyond the confines of the film, influencing subsequent portrayals of athletes in cinema.

Vulnerability as a Strength:

In a landscape where sports heroes are often celebrated for their physical prowess and stoic resilience, Nolte's Phil Elliott introduces vulnerability as a strength. The character's struggles with pain, addiction, and the existential angst of a waning career humanize him, making him more relatable to audiences. Nolte's portrayal challenges the notion that vulnerability diminishes the stature of an athlete, asserting that it is an integral part of the human experience, even for those in the spotlight.

Relatable Struggles Beyond the Field:

Nolte's performance extends beyond the football field, exploring the relatable struggles faced by athletes in their personal lives. Phil Elliott's relationships, his attempts to find meaning beyond football, and his confrontation with societal expectations resonate with universal themes. By humanizing the athlete, Nolte transcends the limitations of the sports genre, creating a character whose struggles extend into the broader canvas of the human condition.

Impact on Nolte's Career:

The success of "North Dallas Forty" and Nick Nolte's breakthrough role had a profound impact on the trajectory of his career. The film marked a turning point, propelling Nolte from a talented actor to a leading man capable of commanding complex and challenging roles. The authenticity and depth he brought to Phil Elliott showcased his range as an actor, laying the foundation for a career that would span decades and encompass a diverse array of characters.

Leading Man Status:

Following "North Dallas Forty," Nolte's leading man status was solidified, and he became a sought-after actor for roles that demanded emotional depth and complexity. The success of the film demonstrated that audiences were hungry for performances that defied stereotypes and embraced the messiness of the human experience. Nolte's ability to navigate the intricacies of Phil Elliott set the stage for a career marked by memorable portrayals and a willingness to tackle challenging and unconventional roles.

Diverse Range of Characters:

The impact of Nolte's breakthrough role is evident in the diverse range of characters he would go on to portray. From the brooding detective in "48 Hrs." (1982) to the tormented Vietnam War veteran in "The Prince of Tides" (1991), Nolte's career trajectory showcases a willingness to explore characters with depth, nuance, and emotional complexity. The legacy of his breakthrough role is woven into the fabric of his filmography, influencing the types of roles he would choose in the years to come.

Cultural Relevance and Enduring Legacy:

Nick Nolte's breakthrough role in "North Dallas Forty" endures as a culturally relevant and resonant portrayal of the athlete as a multifaceted human being. The film's impact extends beyond its initial release, leaving an indelible mark on the cultural conversation surrounding sports, identity, and the price of success.

Championing Authenticity in Sports Cinema:

"North Dallas Forty" and Nolte's performance stand as champions of authenticity in sports cinema. The film's refusal to conform to idealized heroism and its willingness to confront systemic issues within professional football set a standard for future sports dramas. Nolte's portrayal of Phil Elliott becomes a touchstone for actors and filmmakers who seek to explore the complexities of athletic characters with honesty and depth.

Influence on Subsequent Sports Films:

The influence of Nolte's breakthrough role is evident in subsequent sports films that followed a similar path of authenticity and nuance. Movies such as "The Wrestler" (2008) and "Foxcatcher" (2014) owe a debt to "North Dallas Forty" for paving the way to more realistic and emotionally rich portrayals of athletes. The film's legacy reverberates in the willingness of filmmakers to delve into the personal and psychological dimensions of sports narratives.

Continued Reverence for Phil Elliott:

Phil Elliott remains an enduring and revered character in the pantheon of sports cinema. Nolte's portrayal ensured that the character would not be relegated to the sidelines of cinematic history but would continue to be discussed and analyzed for its cultural impact. The film's portrayal of the athlete as a complex and flawed individual continues to resonate with audiences who appreciate narratives that challenge and expand the conventions of the genre.

Conclusion: Nolte's Enduring Legacy in "North Dallas Forty":

As we conclude our exploration of Nick Nolte's breakthrough role in "North Dallas Forty," we unveil a performance that transcends the boundaries of sports cinema. Nolte's portrayal of Phil Elliott goes beyond the football field, offering a window into the complexities of the human experience. The actor's ability to humanize the athlete, confront systemic injustices, and defy conventions laid the groundwork for a career marked by authenticity, range, and cultural impact.

"North Dallas Forty" stands as a testament to the transformative power of an actor fully embodying a character. Nolte's portrayal of Phil Elliott remains a touchstone for those who seek to explore the intricacies of identity, purpose, and the toll of success within the framework of sports narratives. As we continue our cinematic journey through the chapters that follow, we carry with us the enduring legacy of Nick Nolte's breakthrough role—a legacy that resonates far beyond the confines of the football field and continues to shape the landscape of sports cinema.

## Mature Themes Explore Football's Toll

In the realm of sports cinema, where narratives often gravitate toward triumph, heroism, and the glory of victory, "North Dallas Forty" (1979) stands as a stark departure. Ted Kotcheff's film, based on Peter Gent's semi-autobiographical novel, transcends the boundaries of traditional football movies by delving into mature themes that candidly explore the toll exacted by the sport on its athletes. As we dissect the narrative layers of "North Dallas Forty," we unravel a film that confronts the harsh realities of professional football, navigating themes of physical and emotional pain, the use of substances to cope, and the psychological toll of a relentless pursuit of success.

The Brutal Physicality of Football:

"North Dallas Forty" opens with a declaration that reverberates throughout the film: football is not a contact sport; it's a collision sport. This statement becomes a thematic cornerstone as the movie immerses viewers in the brutal physicality of the sport, stripping away the veneer of glamour associated with professional football. The film's unflinching portrayal of bone-crushing tackles, on-field injuries, and the toll exacted on players' bodies serves as a commentary on the sacrifice required to compete at the highest level.

Reality of Injuries: One of the mature themes explored in "North Dallas Forty" is the stark reality of injuries in professional football. The film goes beyond the superficial depiction of players shaking off injuries and glorifies the physical toll that each game exacts. Through graphic scenes and candid portrayals, the narrative underscores that the pursuit of victory often comes at a cost—broken bones, torn ligaments, and a constant battle against pain.

Pain as a Constant Companion: A recurring motif in the film is the omnipresence of pain. Players are shown relying on painkillers to numb their bodies, highlighting the normalization of pain as an inherent part of the athlete's experience. The narrative thrusts the audience into a visceral understanding of the physical toll, portraying pain not as a momentary inconvenience but as a constant companion that athletes must navigate to continue competing.

Substance Abuse as Coping Mechanism:

"North Dallas Forty" ventures into mature territory by addressing the use of substances as a coping mechanism within the high-stakes world of professional football. The film unflinchingly portrays the pervasive use of painkillers, alcohol, and other substances as a means for players to manage the physical and emotional toll of their profession.

Painkillers and Self-Medication: The film provides an unfiltered glimpse into the culture of self-medication prevalent among players. Scenes depicting players sharing painkillers, injecting themselves with substances, and numbing their bodies to endure the rigors of the sport shed light on the precarious line between maintaining peak physical performance and succumbing to the inevitable toll on the body.

Escapism Through Substance Use: "North Dallas Forty" explores the theme of escapism through substance use—a means for players to temporarily escape the physical pain, the pressure to perform, and the existential questions that loom over their careers. This mature exploration challenges traditional sports movie narratives that often shy away from depicting the less glamorous aspects of athletes' lives.

Psychological Toll of the Relentless Pursuit:

Beyond the physical toll, the film ventures into the psychological challenges faced by athletes in the relentless pursuit of success. The pressure to conform, the fear of career-ending injuries, and the existential questions that arise when an athlete confronts the limits of their physical abilities become central themes that elevate "North Dallas Forty" into a character study of profound depth.

Fear of Career-Ending Injuries: The fear of career-ending injuries looms large in the minds of the characters. The narrative explores the psychological impact of knowing that one wrong move on the field could spell the end of a player's career. This fear permeates the locker room, creating an atmosphere of anxiety and paranoia that adds a layer of tension to the film.

Existential Questions and Identity Crisis: "North Dallas Forty" does not shy away from delving into the existential questions that plague athletes as they navigate the later stages of their careers. The film poses poignant inquiries about identity beyond the game—Who are these athletes when stripped of their football personas? What happens when the cheers fade, and the stadium lights dim? The exploration of an identity crisis becomes a mature theme that resonates beyond the football field.

The Broader Societal Context:

In its mature exploration of football's toll, "North Dallas Forty" also invites viewers to consider the broader societal context in which professional athletes operate. The film touches on issues such as the commodification of players, the dehumanizing nature of the sports industry, and the expectations imposed on athletes to conform to a particular image.

Commodification of Players: The narrative confronts the commodification of players within the sports industry, depicting them as assets to be managed, traded, and discarded based on their perceived value to the team. The film questions the ethics of an industry that places a premium on performance while disregarding the long-term well-being of its athletes.

Dehumanization Within the Sports Industry: "North Dallas Forty" pulls back the curtain on the dehumanizing aspects of the sports industry. The pressures exerted by team management, the lack of job security, and the expectation for players to prioritize the team's success over personal well-being contribute to an environment where athletes are reduced to commodities rather than individuals.

Impact on Subsequent Sports Films:

The mature themes explored in "North Dallas Forty" had a profound impact on subsequent sports films, influencing the trajectory of the genre toward more nuanced and realistic portrayals of athletes. The film's willingness to confront the less glamorous aspects of professional sports paved the way for a new wave of narratives that challenged audience expectations.

Shift Toward Realism: The film's commitment to realism over idealism set a standard for subsequent sports dramas. Filmmakers began to move away from formulaic narratives of triumph over adversity and embraced storytelling that reflected the messy, complex realities faced by athletes. "North Dallas Forty" championed a shift toward authenticity, influencing filmmakers to explore the psychological, physical, and societal dimensions of sports narratives.

Exploration of Athlete Vulnerability: The mature exploration of football's toll in "North Dallas Forty" opened the door for a deeper exploration of athlete vulnerability in sports cinema. Subsequent films, such as "Jerry Maguire" (1996) and "The Wrestler" (2008), delved into the personal struggles of athletes, depicting characters who grapple with the consequences of their chosen profession beyond the playing field.

Conclusion: Navigating Mature Terrain with Authenticity:

As we conclude our exploration of "North Dallas Forty," we recognize the film's pioneering journey into mature terrain within sports cinema. The narrative's unfiltered portrayal of the physical, psychological, and societal toll exacted by professional football challenged the conventions of the genre. Through its commitment to authenticity, the film not only paved the way for a more nuanced understanding of the athlete's experience but also left an enduring impact on the landscape of sports dramas.

"North Dallas Forty" serves as a cinematic touchstone, inviting audiences to confront the harsh realities that coexist with the glory of victory on the football field. The mature themes explored within its narrative continue to resonate, reminding us that the pursuit of success in professional sports is a complex and multifaceted journey—one that transcends the boundaries of the game and delves into the very essence of the human experience.

## The Lingering Impact on Sports Dramas

"North Dallas Forty" (1979) isn't just a film; it's a seismic shift in the landscape of sports cinema. As we examine the cinematic reverberations of Ted Kotcheff's exploration of the gritty underbelly of professional football, we uncover the enduring impact the film has had on the trajectory of sports dramas. From its unflinching portrayal of the less glamorous aspects of athletes' lives to its defiance of conventional hero narratives, "North Dallas Forty" laid the groundwork for a new era in sports cinema—one marked by authenticity, complexity, and a willingness to navigate mature themes.

Challenging the Heroic Paradigm:

At the heart of "North Dallas Forty's" impact on sports dramas lies its defiance against the heroic paradigm that had long dominated the genre. Traditionally, sports films followed a formulaic arc, where athletes triumphed over adversity, achieved glory on the field, and emerged as unblemished heroes. "North Dallas Forty" shattered this paradigm, presenting audiences with a protagonist, Phil Elliott, who defied the idealized image of the sports hero.

Complexity Over Simplicity: The film introduced a level of complexity to its characters that went beyond the simplistic hero-villain dichotomy. Phil Elliott, portrayed with raw authenticity by Nick Nolte, became a multifaceted antihero—a player grappling with internal demons, the physical toll of the sport, and the pressures to conform. This departure from the conventional hero's journey marked a turning point in sports cinema, challenging filmmakers to embrace the messiness and contradictions inherent in athletes' lives.

Resistance to Easy Resolutions: "North Dallas Forty" resisted the temptation to provide easy resolutions to its characters' struggles. Unlike traditional sports films where victory on the field equated to personal redemption, this narrative chose to leave certain conflicts unresolved. The film's refusal to tie up every narrative thread neatly echoed the unpredictability and complexity of real-life sports stories, laying the foundation for a more realistic and nuanced portrayal of athletes in subsequent films.

Nuanced Portrayal of Athlete Struggles:

The film's impact on sports dramas extends beyond its narrative choices to its nuanced portrayal of the struggles faced by athletes both on and off the field. "North Dallas Forty" humanized its characters, shedding light on the less glamorous aspects of their lives and challenging the sanitized image often associated with sports heroes.

Physical Toll and Injury Realities: "North Dallas Forty" forced audiences to confront the harsh physical toll that professional football exacts on its players. Through graphic depictions of injuries, pain management, and the pervasive use of substances, the film peeled back the curtain on the toll that athletes pay to compete at the highest level. This candid exploration of the physical realities of the sport set a precedent for a more realistic portrayal of athletes in subsequent films.

Psychological Challenges and Identity Crisis: The film delved into the psychological challenges faced by athletes, exploring themes of identity crisis, existential questioning, and the fear of a career-ending injury. By presenting athletes as individuals grappling with personal and emotional complexities, "North Dallas Forty" paved the way for sports dramas that embraced the psychological dimensions of their characters. The narrative authenticity encouraged filmmakers to move beyond surface-level storytelling and delve into the internal struggles that define athletes' experiences.

Paving the Way for Subversive Sports Dramas:

"North Dallas Forty" challenged not only the content but also the stylistic and tonal conventions of sports dramas. The film's subversive approach to storytelling opened the door for filmmakers to experiment with new narrative techniques, inject darker tones, and explore the genre's potential for social critique.

Documentary-Like Realism: One of the distinctive features of "North Dallas Forty" was its documentary-like realism. The handheld camera work and unfiltered portrayal of locker room dynamics lent the film an authenticity that resonated with audiences. This stylistic choice, influenced by the burgeoning documentary movement of the time, set a precedent for sports films to embrace a more immersive and realistic visual language.

Social Commentary Through Sports: The film's willingness to address systemic issues within the sports industry positioned it as a vehicle for social commentary. "North Dallas Forty" tackled themes of commodification, dehumanization, and the exploitation of athletes—a departure from the celebratory narratives that often characterized sports films. This subversive element laid the groundwork for subsequent sports dramas that sought to critique societal structures through the lens of athletics.

Influence on Character-Driven Sports Narratives:

"North Dallas Forty" marked a shift in focus from the spectacle of the game to the intimate exploration of characters navigating the challenges of their chosen profession. This emphasis on character-driven narratives became a hallmark of the film and influenced a generation of sports dramas that prioritized the internal journeys of their protagonists.

Nick Nolte's Breakthrough Performance: Central to the film's character-driven approach was Nick Nolte's breakthrough performance as Phil Elliott. Nolte's portrayal transcended the boundaries of sports cinema, transforming Elliott into a character study of profound depth. This emphasis on character nuance and the actor's ability to convey the internal struggles of the athlete set a standard for sports dramas that followed.

Legacy of Multifaceted Athletes: "North Dallas Forty" introduced audiences to the concept of the multifaceted athlete—a character who exists beyond the confines of the playing field. This legacy is evident in subsequent sports films that have sought to explore the broader lives, vulnerabilities, and personal challenges faced by athletes. The film's influence is seen in narratives that resist reducing athletes to one-dimensional heroes and instead celebrate their humanity.

Cinematic Exploration of Athlete Rebellion:

The film's narrative, centered around Phil Elliott's resistance to the constraints imposed by the sports industry, became a template for cinematic explorations of athlete rebellion. "North Dallas Forty" laid the groundwork for stories that challenge the status quo, question authority, and highlight the tensions between players and the institutions that govern their careers.

Confrontation with Systemic Injustices: Phil Elliott's defiance against the systemic injustices within professional football became a narrative thread that resonated with audiences. This confrontation with authority, whether it be team management, league officials, or societal expectations, set a precedent for sports films that explore the conflicts between athletes and the institutions that control their destinies.

Impact on Later Sports Rebellion Narratives: The film's influence on later sports rebellion narratives is evident in movies like "Jerry Maguire" (1996), "Remember the Titans" (2000), and "Moneyball" (2011). These films echo "North Dallas Forty's" themes of challenging established norms, advocating for individual agency, and resisting the dehumanization inherent in the sports industry.

Cultural Relevance and Enduring Conversations:

More than four decades after its release, "North Dallas Forty" remains a cultural touchstone that continues to inspire conversations about the intersection of sports and cinema. The film's enduring relevance lies not only in its impact on subsequent sports dramas but also in its ability to provoke discussions about the ethical, moral, and personal dimensions of the sports world.

Legacy in Conversations About Athlete Well-Being: The film's legacy is intertwined with ongoing conversations about athlete well-being, the price of success, and the responsibilities of sports institutions. "North Dallas Forty" sparked a dialogue that transcends the boundaries of cinema, prompting discussions about the treatment of athletes, the impact of injuries, and the broader societal expectations placed on those in the spotlight.

Continued Analysis of Systemic Issues: As sports dramas continue to evolve, "North Dallas Forty" remains a benchmark for filmmakers and audiences alike. The film's unapologetic examination of systemic issues within the sports industry—commodification, dehumanization, and the sacrifices demanded of athletes—encourages continued analysis of the broader implications of the games we celebrate.

Conclusion: Redefining the Game of Sports Cinema:

As we reflect on the lingering impact of "North Dallas Forty" on sports dramas, we recognize its role as a game-changer that redefined the rules of the genre. The film's legacy extends beyond its critical acclaim and box office success; it resides in the new era it ushered in—one marked by authenticity, complexity, and a willingness to confront the uncomfortable truths of the sports world.

"North Dallas Forty" stands as a testament to the transformative power of cinema in shaping cultural conversations. Its influence is felt not only in the films that followed but also in the broader discussions about the intersection of sports, identity, and societal expectations. As we navigate the chapters that follow, we carry with us the enduring legacy of a film that dared to challenge, provoke, and redefine the game of sports cinema.

## Chapter 3: Brian's Song (1971)
## The Tearjerker That Caught the NFL By Surprise

In the realm of sports cinema, few films elicit the emotional resonance and enduring impact of "Brian's Song" (1971). Directed by Buzz Kulik, this made-for-television movie transcended its small screen origins to become a cultural touchstone. As we delve into the subtopic "The Tearjerker That Caught the NFL By Surprise," we unravel the emotional journey of the film, the unexpected response it garnered from the National Football League (NFL), and its lasting legacy as a poignant exploration of friendship, loss, and the indomitable spirit that defines the game of football.

Setting the Stage: A Different Kind of Football Film:

In the landscape of football cinema, which often celebrated the triumphs on the field, "Brian's Song" arrived as a departure from the norm. Based on the real-life friendship between Brian Piccolo and Gale Sayers, two players on the Chicago Bears in the 1960s, the film took a heartfelt and introspective approach, focusing not solely on the sport itself but on the profound impact of camaraderie and brotherhood.

Adaptation of Sayers' Memoir: The source material for the film was Gale Sayers' memoir, "I Am Third," co-written with Al Silverman. Rather than providing a standard sports narrative, the memoir delved into the depth of Sayers' friendship with Brian Piccolo and the challenges they faced together, both on and off the field. The decision to adapt this memoir for the screen marked the beginning of a cinematic journey that would resonate far beyond the expectations of the NFL and the audience.

Unexpected Emotional Resonance:

"Brian's Song" premiered on ABC on November 30, 1971, and what followed was nothing short of a cultural phenomenon. The film, which was initially intended as a television movie, resonated deeply with audiences, surprising both critics and the NFL establishment with its emotional intensity and powerful storytelling.

The Friendship that Transcended: At its core, "Brian's Song" was a testament to the transcendent power of friendship. The film chronicled the bond between Gale Sayers, played by Billy Dee Williams, and Brian Piccolo, portrayed by James Caan, as they navigated the challenges of professional football, racial tensions, and ultimately, Piccolo's battle with terminal cancer. The genuine chemistry between Williams and Caan, coupled with their authentic performances, elevated the film beyond the confines of a traditional sports narrative.

Breaking Racial Barriers: One of the aspects that caught the NFL by surprise was the film's unflinching exploration of racial tensions. In the 1960s, professional football, like much of American society, was grappling with racial integration. "Brian's Song" tackled this issue head-on, portraying the genuine friendship between Sayers, an African American player, and Piccolo, a Caucasian player, at a time when racial divides were still prevalent in the sports world. The film's willingness to confront racial issues set it apart from other football dramas of the era.

Piccolo's Battle with Cancer: The emotional core of the film emerged as Brian Piccolo faced a devastating diagnosis of cancer. The narrative shifted from the football field to the deeply personal struggles of a young man confronting mortality. Piccolo's battle became a universal story of courage, resilience, and the enduring human spirit. The unexpected emotional weight of the film left audiences in tears and prompted a profound reevaluation of what a football movie could be.

The NFL's Reaction: Surprise and Support:

The National Football League, known for its focus on the physical prowess and competitive nature of the sport, was initially taken aback by the emotional impact of "Brian's Song." The film's departure from the conventional sports narrative prompted a reassessment of the genre's potential to connect with audiences on a deeply emotional level.

An Unprecedented Response: The NFL, accustomed to films that celebrated the athleticism and triumphs of its players, had not anticipated the emotional resonance that "Brian's Song" would evoke. The league, which often sought to control its public image, found itself navigating uncharted territory as the film's emotional depth sparked conversations that extended beyond the gridiron.

Recognition of Human Stories: While the NFL was surprised by the film's emotional impact, it soon recognized the value of telling human stories that transcended the on-field exploits. "Brian's Song" became a catalyst for a shift in the league's approach to media and storytelling. The unexpected success of the film paved the way for future projects that delved into the personal lives, struggles, and triumphs of its players.

Legacy Beyond the Gridiron:

The legacy of "Brian's Song" extends far beyond its initial broadcast. The film's impact on sports cinema, its influence on the NFL's approach to storytelling, and its enduring relevance in popular culture all contribute to its status as a seminal work in the genre.

Reevaluation of Football Narratives: "Brian's Song" prompted a reevaluation of football narratives in cinema. It demonstrated that audiences were receptive to stories that went beyond the game itself, stories that explored the human experiences of the athletes. The film paved the way for a more diverse range of football stories, from character-driven dramas to explorations of social issues within the sport.

Humanizing Football Icons: The film's success contributed to a broader trend of humanizing football icons. It showed that audiences were not only interested in the physical prowess of players but also in their vulnerabilities, relationships, and personal journeys. This shift in perspective influenced subsequent football films that sought to capture the multifaceted lives of those who played the game.

Cultural Impact:

"Brian's Song" left an indelible mark on the cultural landscape. Its influence extends beyond the realms of sports and cinema, touching on themes of friendship, resilience, and the enduring impact of personal connections.

Cultural Touchstone for Friendship: The film became a cultural touchstone for friendship, resonating with audiences on a deeply emotional level. The portrayal of the bond between Gale Sayers and Brian Piccolo transcended the football field, becoming a symbol of enduring friendship that has left a lasting impact on how such relationships are portrayed in popular culture.

Perpetual Tearjerker: Decades after its release, "Brian's Song" remains a perpetual tearjerker. The film's ability to evoke genuine emotion and empathy has solidified its place in the pantheon of cinematic tearjerkers. Scenes from the film, particularly those depicting Piccolo's illness and the poignant moments between the two friends, continue to be referenced and remembered by audiences.

Conclusion: An Unexpected Masterpiece:

As we conclude our exploration of "Brian's Song" and its surprising impact on the NFL and sports cinema, we recognize the film as an unexpected masterpiece that defied expectations and redefined the possibilities of the football genre. The tearjerker that caught the NFL by surprise has left an enduring legacy, not only for its emotional resonance but also for its role in ushering in a new era of football storytelling—one that embraces the humanity, vulnerability, and enduring spirit of those who play the game.

## Unlikely Friendship Between Sayers and Piccolo

In the realm of sports narratives, where tales of fierce competition and triumph often take center stage, "Brian's Song" (1971) stands apart as a poignant exploration of an unlikely friendship that transcends the boundaries of the football field. Directed by Buzz Kulik and based on Gale Sayers' memoir "I Am Third," the film delves into the deep and enduring bond between two Chicago Bears players, Gale Sayers and Brian Piccolo. As we explore the subtopic of their "Unlikely Friendship," we unravel the complexities, challenges, and enduring impact of a relationship that defied societal norms and racial expectations of its time.

Setting the Stage: Football, Friendship, and Racial Dynamics:

The backdrop of the 1960s, a tumultuous period in American history marked by racial tensions and social upheaval, serves as the canvas upon which the friendship between Gale Sayers and Brian Piccolo unfolds. Against the backdrop of a changing America and the racially divided landscape of professional football, the friendship between Sayers, an African American running back, and Piccolo, a Caucasian running back, becomes a microcosm of the broader societal shifts taking place.

The Racial Landscape of the NFL: In the 1960s, the National Football League (NFL) was grappling with the challenges of racial integration. The league, like much of American society, was in the midst of a transformative period where African American players were breaking through longstanding racial barriers. "Brian's Song" navigates this racial landscape, providing a lens through which to examine the evolving dynamics within the NFL and society at large.

Breaking Racial Barriers: The friendship between Sayers and Piccolo becomes a symbol of breaking racial barriers. At a time when racial tensions were palpable both on and off the field, their camaraderie challenged the status quo. The film captures the initial unease, skepticism, and outright resistance that the two players face as they form an alliance that extends beyond the game.

The Birth of Friendship: From Teammates to Brothers:

The film chronicles the evolution of the friendship between Gale Sayers, portrayed by Billy Dee Williams, and Brian Piccolo, played by James Caan. Beginning as teammates on the Chicago Bears, their relationship transforms from a professional alliance to a deep and meaningful friendship, defying societal expectations and racial norms.

Teammates in a Divided Era: As professional football players in the racially divided landscape of the 1960s, Sayers and Piccolo initially navigate their roles as teammates in a sport where racial integration was a nascent and sometimes contentious development. The film captures the initial wariness, cultural differences, and the racial dynamics at play as they become part of a team that reflects the broader societal changes.

The Catalyst: A Shared Goal: What initially brings Sayers and Piccolo together is their shared goal of becoming successful football players. Despite their different backgrounds and experiences, the common ground of pursuing excellence on the field serves as the catalyst for their burgeoning friendship. Football becomes the crucible in which their bond is forged, laying the foundation for a relationship that extends far beyond the parameters of the game.

Beyond Race: A Brotherhood Forms: "Brian's Song" skillfully navigates the complexities of race by portraying the friendship between Sayers and Piccolo as one that transcends skin color. As they face adversity together, both on and off the field, the film emphasizes the common humanity that unites them. The racial barriers that initially framed their interactions slowly erode, giving way to a deep sense of brotherhood that becomes the emotional core of the narrative.

Shared Triumphs and Personal Struggles:

The strength of the friendship between Sayers and Piccolo is tested not only by external pressures but also by the personal triumphs and struggles each player faces. The film weaves a narrative tapestry that explores the highs and lows of their individual journeys and how their friendship serves as a source of support and understanding.

On-Field Triumphs: As they achieve success on the football field, Sayers and Piccolo become emblematic of the potential for unity and camaraderie in a racially diverse team. The film captures their on-field triumphs, highlighting their individual skills and the collective strength of the Chicago Bears. The shared victories become moments of celebration for a friendship that defies the expectations of a racially divided society.

Off-Field Challenges: The strength of their friendship is tested when Piccolo is diagnosed with terminal cancer. The off-field challenges become a crucible that illuminates the depth of their bond. Sayers becomes a pillar of support for Piccolo as he faces the physical and emotional toll of his illness. The film navigates the complexities of friendship in the face of adversity, portraying the genuine care, empathy, and sacrifices that define their relationship.

Navigating Racial Dynamics:

"Brian's Song" not only depicts the friendship between Sayers and Piccolo but also delves into the racial dynamics that shape their interactions, both within the team and in the broader societal context.

Team Dynamics and Racial Tensions: Within the Chicago Bears, the film reflects the racial tensions and challenges that existed in professional football during the 1960s. The locker room becomes a microcosm of societal attitudes, with initial resistance and skepticism from some teammates. The film does not shy away from portraying the racial divide that characterized the era, providing a nuanced exploration of how race influenced relationships within the team.

Friendship as a Catalyst for Change: Sayers and Piccolo's friendship becomes a catalyst for change within the team. As their genuine camaraderie becomes evident, it challenges the preconceived notions of their teammates. The film suggests that the power of friendship has the potential to transcend racial boundaries and reshape the dynamics of a team.

The Emotional Impact: From Locker Room to Living Rooms:

As "Brian's Song" was broadcast on television screens across America, its emotional impact reverberated beyond the confines of the football field. The unexpected emotional resonance of the film made it a cultural phenomenon and transformed it into a shared experience for audiences of diverse backgrounds.

Unexpected Tears: The emotional depth of "Brian's Song" took audiences by surprise. Viewers who tuned in expecting a typical football drama found themselves emotionally moved by the genuine affection and camaraderie between Sayers and Piccolo. The film's ability to evoke tears, even from those who may not have been avid football fans, spoke to its universal themes of friendship, resilience, and the human experience.

Cultural Conversations: The emotional impact of the film extended beyond individual reactions to become a topic of cultural conversations. Viewers found themselves discussing the film with friends, family, and colleagues, creating a shared cultural experience. The unexpected emotional resonance sparked discussions about friendship, mortality, and the enduring impact of personal connections.

Legacy of Friendship:

The friendship between Gale Sayers and Brian Piccolo left an enduring legacy, both within the narrative of "Brian's Song" and in the broader cultural consciousness. The film's portrayal of an unlikely friendship continues to resonate and inspire, leaving an indelible mark on the landscape of sports cinema.

Inspiration for Future Narratives: The friendship depicted in "Brian's Song" became an inspiration for future narratives in sports cinema. Filmmakers and storytellers looked to the film as a benchmark for authentic portrayals of friendships that transcend societal expectations. The legacy of Sayers and Piccolo's bond can be seen in subsequent films that explore the personal relationships between athletes.

Cultural Impact Beyond Football: Beyond the realm of football, the friendship between Sayers and Piccolo had a cultural impact that reverberated across different spheres. The film's exploration of camaraderie, empathy, and the ability of friendship to transcend societal divisions resonated with audiences who saw in Sayers and Piccolo a reflection of their own shared humanity.

Conclusion: Beyond the Game, Beyond the Screen:

As we reflect on the unlikely friendship between Gale Sayers and Brian Piccolo in "Brian's Song," we recognize its significance not only as a narrative element within the film but as a cultural touchstone that transcends the boundaries of the football field. The film's exploration of an authentic and enduring bond challenges stereotypes, navigates racial dynamics, and leaves an enduring legacy as a testament to the power of friendship. Beyond the game and beyond the screen, the friendship between Sayers and Piccolo stands as a poignant reminder of the shared humanity that unites us all.

### Breaking Barriers On and Off the Field

"Brian's Song" (1971) emerges as a timeless cinematic exploration that extends beyond the gridiron, transcending the conventional boundaries of sports films. At its heart is a narrative that goes beyond the on-field exploits of athletes, delving into the profound impact of friendship, resilience, and the breaking of societal barriers. This chapter explores how the film, directed by Buzz Kulik and based on Gale Sayers' memoir "I Am Third," navigates the complexities of breaking barriers, both on and off the football field.

Setting the Stage: Societal Barriers of the 1960s:

In the backdrop of the 1960s—a decade marked by civil rights struggles, societal upheavals, and shifting cultural dynamics—"Brian's Song" emerges as a poignant narrative that mirrors the societal barriers of its time. Racial tensions were palpable, and institutionalized segregation still cast a shadow over various aspects of American life, including the world of professional football.

The NFL's Racial Landscape: The National Football League (NFL), like many institutions, was navigating the complexities of racial integration. The league's racial landscape mirrored the broader societal struggles for equality and inclusion. Against this backdrop, the friendship between Gale Sayers, an African American running back, and Brian Piccolo, a Caucasian running back, becomes a narrative thread that not only defies racial stereotypes but challenges societal norms.

Breaking Racial Barriers:

"Brian's Song" positions itself as a narrative that actively seeks to break racial barriers, challenging preconceived notions about race relations both on and off the football field.

Teammates Beyond Color: As Sayers and Piccolo become teammates on the Chicago Bears, the film subtly and powerfully communicates the breaking down of racial barriers within the confines of the team. The locker room, traditionally a microcosm of societal attitudes, becomes a space where individuals are defined by their shared pursuit of excellence rather than the color of their skin.

Friendship as a Catalyst for Change: The friendship between Sayers and Piccolo becomes a catalyst for change within the team and, by extension, within the narrative itself. The film suggests that genuine camaraderie and friendship have the power to transcend racial boundaries, challenging stereotypes and reshaping the dynamics of a team. This thematic exploration goes beyond the typical sports film narrative, positioning "Brian's Song" as a transformative cinematic work.

Navigating Interracial Friendship:

The film navigates the complexities of interracial friendship during a period when such relationships were met with resistance, skepticism, and societal scrutiny.

Unease and Skepticism: The initial stages of Sayers and Piccolo's friendship are marked by a palpable unease and skepticism. This mirrors the racial tensions of the time, where interracial friendships were often met with societal resistance. The film does not shy away from portraying the challenges the two players face as they navigate the uncharted territory of a deep, meaningful connection that goes beyond racial divides.

Authenticity Amidst Challenges: "Brian's Song" authentically depicts the challenges faced by Sayers and Piccolo as they forge an authentic friendship. Whether it's the skepticism of teammates or the societal expectations that questioned the legitimacy of their bond, the film navigates these challenges with sensitivity and realism. The authenticity of their friendship becomes a testament to the film's commitment to portraying the complexities of breaking racial barriers.

The Impact of Personal Bonds:

Beyond the societal implications, "Brian's Song" underscores the profound impact of personal bonds formed between individuals who, on the surface, may seem worlds apart.

The Power of Friendship: The film presents friendship as a powerful force capable of transcending societal expectations. Sayers and Piccolo's connection becomes a source of mutual support, understanding, and shared triumphs. The depth of their friendship challenges the conventional narrative of racial divisions, offering a vision of unity that goes beyond the limitations of societal norms.

Shared Triumphs, Shared Struggles: As Sayers and Piccolo navigate the challenges of professional football, their shared triumphs and struggles become emblematic of the common human experience. The film's narrative goes beyond racial dynamics to explore the universal themes of friendship, resilience, and the enduring spirit that defines the game of football.

Navigating Personal and Professional Challenges:

"Brian's Song" skillfully intertwines personal and professional challenges, using them as a backdrop to explore the breaking of barriers within the narrative.

On-Field Excellence: The film celebrates the on-field excellence of both Sayers and Piccolo, showcasing their individual skills and contributions to the Chicago Bears. In doing so, it challenges stereotypes about racial capabilities and athleticism. By highlighting the prowess of these athletes, the film contributes to breaking down racial barriers within the context of the sport.

Off-Field Adversity: The narrative takes a poignant turn when Piccolo is diagnosed with terminal cancer. The off-field adversity becomes a crucible that not only tests the strength of their friendship but also challenges societal expectations. Piccolo's illness becomes a universal story of courage, resilience, and the indomitable human spirit, breaking through the barriers of race and sports expectations.

Impact on Team Dynamics:

"Brian's Song" explores how the breaking of racial barriers within the friendship of Sayers and Piccolo influences the dynamics of the team.

Changing Attitudes in the Locker Room: As the film progresses, the attitudes within the locker room evolve. The initially skeptical teammates witness the authenticity and depth of the friendship between Sayers and Piccolo. This transformation within the team becomes a microcosm of the broader societal shift happening outside the confines of the football field.

Friendship as a Unifying Force: The friendship between Sayers and Piccolo emerges as a unifying force within the team. The film subtly suggests that breaking racial barriers not only challenges stereotypes but also fosters unity and camaraderie. The team becomes a diverse collective where individual strengths, regardless of race, contribute to the collective success.

Cultural Impact Beyond Football:

"Brian's Song" leaves an enduring cultural impact, transcending the realm of football to become a touchstone for discussions about breaking societal barriers.

Inspiration for Conversations: The film becomes an inspiration for conversations about breaking racial barriers and the power of genuine human connections. Viewers find themselves discussing not only the dynamics within the film but also how the narrative resonates with broader societal aspirations for unity and understanding.

Cultural Conversations About Friendship: The friendship between Sayers and Piccolo becomes a cultural reference point for discussions about friendship that transcends societal divisions. The film prompts conversations about the importance of genuine connections and the potential for personal relationships to influence broader societal attitudes.

Legacy of Breaking Barriers:

As we reflect on "Brian's Song" and its narrative exploration of breaking barriers, it becomes evident that the film's legacy extends far beyond the screen.

Influence on Subsequent Narratives: The film's portrayal of breaking racial barriers within the context of friendship influences subsequent narratives in sports cinema. Filmmakers look to "Brian's Song" as a benchmark for authentic portrayals of relationships that challenge societal norms and contribute to a more inclusive storytelling landscape.

Broader Impact on Sports Culture: Beyond the realm of cinema, "Brian's Song" contributes to a broader impact on sports culture. The film, by depicting the breaking of racial barriers within the context of professional football, becomes a part of a larger narrative about the evolving dynamics of racial inclusion within sports.

Conclusion: A Cinematic Catalyst for Change:

In conclusion, "Brian's Song" emerges as a cinematic catalyst for change, using the narrative of an unlikely friendship to explore and challenge societal barriers. The film's commitment to authenticity, its nuanced portrayal of friendship, and its exploration of breaking racial barriers contribute to its enduring legacy. Beyond the game of football, "Brian's Song" becomes a timeless exploration of the transformative power of personal connections and the potential for genuine friendships to break down the barriers that divide us.

## New Perspective on Black Athletes

"Brian's Song" (1971) not only stands as a testament to the power of friendship but also serves as a pivotal work in cinema that offers a new perspective on black athletes. In an era marked by racial tensions and a changing landscape in professional sports, the film, directed by Buzz Kulik and based on Gale Sayers' memoir "I Am Third," emerges as a groundbreaking narrative that goes beyond conventional portrayals of black athletes. This chapter explores the film's contribution to shaping a new perspective on black athletes, navigating the complexities of race, identity, and representation.

Setting the Stage: Racial Dynamics in 1960s Sports:

The 1960s were a period of significant social upheaval and transformation, and the world of professional sports was no exception. Racial dynamics within sports, particularly in the National Football League (NFL), were undergoing a gradual but profound shift. Against this backdrop, "Brian's Song" emerges as a cinematic work that not only reflects the changes in societal attitudes but actively contributes to reshaping the narrative around black athletes.

Breaking Stereotypes:

"Brian's Song" challenges existing stereotypes and preconceived notions about black athletes prevalent in the cinematic and sports landscapes of the time.

Beyond Athleticism: During the 1960s, the portrayal of black athletes in cinema often centered on their physical prowess, emphasizing athleticism over the complexities of their characters. "Brian's Song" disrupts this narrative by presenting black athletes—specifically, Gale Sayers—with a depth and nuance that extends beyond the football field. The film's narrative invites viewers to see Sayers not merely as an athlete but as a multifaceted individual with emotions, vulnerabilities, and a profound capacity for friendship.

Navigating Racial Tensions: The film confronts racial tensions within the context of professional football, acknowledging the challenges faced by black athletes during a period of societal change. Sayers becomes a lens through which the audience explores the complexities of being a black athlete in a predominantly white sports environment. The film neither idealizes nor simplifies these experiences but offers a nuanced portrayal that reflects the realities of the time.

Authentic Portrayal of Black Identity:

"Brian's Song" contributes to a more authentic portrayal of black identity, moving beyond stereotypes to depict the rich tapestry of individual experiences.

Gale Sayers as a Complex Character: Gale Sayers, portrayed by Billy Dee Williams, emerges as a complex and well-rounded character. His identity is not reduced to a set of predetermined attributes but is presented as a combination of talent, ambition, friendship, and personal struggles. The film challenges the one-dimensional representations of black athletes by providing a nuanced and authentic portrayal that reflects the diversity within the black community.

Exploring Personal Narratives: The film encourages audiences to engage with the personal narrative of a black athlete, inviting empathy and understanding. Sayers' journey becomes a vehicle for exploring the universal themes of friendship, resilience, and the human experience. By delving into the personal narrative of a black athlete, "Brian's Song" expands the scope of representation in sports cinema.

Friendship Across Racial Lines:

"Brian's Song" explores the theme of friendship across racial lines, challenging the notion that deep connections can only exist within homogeneous social circles.

Unlikely Bond Between Sayers and Piccolo: The friendship between Gale Sayers and Brian Piccolo becomes a focal point for breaking down racial barriers. The film does not shy away from addressing the initial skepticism and resistance from both sides as the two players form a deep connection. By portraying an unlikely bond between a black and a white athlete, "Brian's Song" challenges the prevailing racial norms and presents a vision of friendship that transcends societal expectations.

Friendship as a Unifying Force: The film suggests that genuine friendship has the power to unite individuals across racial lines. Through the evolving friendship between Sayers and Piccolo, "Brian's Song" promotes a vision of unity and camaraderie that goes beyond the limitations of race. The theme of friendship becomes a powerful vehicle for presenting a new perspective on black athletes—one that emphasizes shared humanity and interconnectedness.

Depiction of Black Athletes in the Media:

"Brian's Song" engages with the broader discourse surrounding the depiction of black athletes in the media, challenging stereotypes perpetuated by mainstream narratives.

Moving Beyond Exploitation: During the 1960s, media portrayals often exploited black athletes, reducing them to simplistic stereotypes or emphasizing physical prowess at the expense of their individuality. "Brian's Song" actively moves beyond this exploitative trend by presenting Gale Sayers as a fully realized individual with emotions, aspirations, and a narrative that extends beyond the sports arena. The film disrupts the prevailing media narrative, offering a more nuanced and humanizing portrayal.

Authenticity in Representation: The film's commitment to authenticity in the representation of black athletes marks a departure from the prevailing norms of the time. By portraying Sayers as a character with agency, emotions, and personal struggles, "Brian's Song" contributes to a more authentic representation of black athletes in the media. The film becomes a landmark work in challenging and reshaping the narrative surrounding black identity within the sports and entertainment industries.

Addressing Racial Dynamics in Professional Football:

"Brian's Song" confronts the racial dynamics present in professional football, providing a lens through which to examine the challenges faced by black athletes within the league.

Navigating Institutional Barriers: The film acknowledges the institutional barriers and racial tensions within professional football during the 1960s. Sayers' journey becomes a narrative thread that allows audiences to witness the challenges faced by black athletes as they navigated a predominantly white sports environment. By addressing these dynamics, "Brian's Song" contributes to a broader conversation about racial inclusion and equity within professional sports.

Professionalism and Racial Identity: Sayers' professionalism and excellence on the field become central to the film's exploration of racial identity. The narrative challenges the notion that a black athlete's success is defined solely by physical prowess, emphasizing instead the importance of skill, dedication, and character. By presenting Sayers as a consummate professional, the film reshapes the discourse around black athletes in professional football.

Impact Beyond the Screen:

The impact of "Brian's Song" extends beyond the cinematic realm, influencing broader conversations about race, identity, and representation.

Cultural Conversations: The film becomes a catalyst for cultural conversations about the representation of black athletes. Audiences engage in discussions about the significance of authentic portrayals, the challenges faced by black athletes, and the potential for media and cinema to shape perceptions. "Brian's Song" prompts a reevaluation of existing stereotypes and encourages a more nuanced understanding of the experiences of black athletes.

Influence on Sports Culture: Beyond its influence on cinema, "Brian's Song" contributes to a shift in sports culture.

The film's narrative resonates with athletes and fans alike, fostering a greater appreciation for the individual stories and struggles of black athletes. By humanizing the experiences of athletes like Gale Sayers, the film becomes a transformative work that leaves a lasting impact on how black athletes are perceived within the broader sports community.

Conclusion: Redefining Narratives, Shaping Perspectives:

As we reflect on "Brian's Song" and its contribution to offering a new perspective on black athletes, it becomes evident that the film transcends its role as a sports drama. The narrative, centered around the friendship of Gale Sayers and Brian Piccolo, becomes a vehicle for challenging stereotypes, addressing racial dynamics, and reshaping the representation of black athletes in the media. Beyond the screen, "Brian's Song" becomes a cultural touchstone, influencing conversations, fostering empathy, and contributing to a more inclusive and authentic portrayal of black athletes in the realms of both cinema and sports.

## Chapter 4: Rudy (1993)
### Bringing Rudy Ruettiger's Inspirational Story to the Big Screen

"Rudy" (1993) stands as a cinematic beacon of inspiration, capturing the hearts of audiences with the true underdog story of Daniel "Rudy" Ruettiger's journey from obscurity to achieving his dream of playing college football at the University of Notre Dame. Directed by David Anspaugh, the film not only chronicles Rudy's tenacity and passion for the game but also brings to life the indomitable spirit that can lead an individual to overcome seemingly insurmountable odds. In this chapter, we delve into the process of bringing Rudy Ruettiger's inspirational story to the big screen, exploring the creative decisions, the portrayal of characters, and the cinematic techniques that transformed a real-life narrative into an enduring symbol of perseverance.

Setting the Stage: The Extraordinary Journey of Rudy Ruettiger:

The early 1990s witnessed a surge in sports films that sought to capture the spirit of true stories, and "Rudy" emerged as a standout example. Against the backdrop of college football and the hallowed grounds of Notre Dame, Rudy Ruettiger's journey provided a compelling narrative that resonated with audiences far beyond the realm of sports.

Adapting Reality for the Screen:

The Genesis of the Project: The decision to bring Rudy Ruettiger's story to the screen was not merely about dramatizing a sports tale but capturing the essence of a young man's unwavering determination. The filmmakers, led by director David Anspaugh and screenwriter Angelo Pizzo, recognized the universal appeal of Rudy's journey—a story that transcended football fandom to become a celebration of human resilience.

Collaboration and Creative Vision: The collaborative effort between Anspaugh and Pizzo was pivotal in shaping the film's creative vision. The challenge lay in distilling Rudy's complex journey into a cinematic narrative that would engage audiences emotionally. The collaboration extended to the casting process, cinematography, and the overall aesthetic of the film, ensuring a cohesive portrayal of Rudy's inspirational odyssey.

The Casting of Sean Astin:

Capturing Rudy's Essence: Central to the success of "Rudy" was the casting of Sean Astin in the titular role. Astin's portrayal went beyond mimicking Rudy's physicality; it captured the essence of Rudy's spirit. Astin brought authenticity to the character, embodying the unwavering determination, the vulnerability, and the infectious passion that defined Rudy's real-life persona.

Physical Transformation: Astin's commitment to the role extended to a physical transformation that mirrored Rudy's journey. Through training and conditioning, Astin not only captured the character's physical prowess but also conveyed the sacrifices and discipline required to pursue a dream against formidable odds.

Building Emotional Resonance:

Personalizing the Journey: "Rudy" succeeded in transforming a sports narrative into a deeply personal and emotional journey. The film eschewed a formulaic approach to focus on the human aspects of Rudy's story—the relationships, the setbacks, and the internal struggles. By humanizing the narrative, the filmmakers ensured that audiences could connect with Rudy on a visceral level, transcending the specific context of college football.

Family Dynamics and Personal Sacrifice: The film delves into Rudy's family dynamics, providing context for his ambition and the challenges he faces. The financial struggles and the sacrifices made by Rudy's working-class family become integral to the emotional fabric of the narrative. This exploration of familial bonds adds layers to Rudy's character, transforming him from a mere underdog to a relatable figure driven by a sense of responsibility and love for his family.

Cinematic Techniques and Notre Dame's Symbolism:

Visual Storytelling: "Rudy" employs visual storytelling techniques to enhance the emotional impact of Rudy's journey. The use of montage sequences, juxtaposed with Rudy's voiceover, allows the audience to witness the progression of his relentless pursuit. Cinematographer Oliver Wood's lens captures the picturesque landscapes of Notre Dame, grounding the film in the iconic setting that symbolizes Rudy's aspirations.

Notre Dame as a Character: The University of Notre Dame becomes a character in its own right, contributing to the film's overarching symbolism. The Gothic architecture, the football tradition, and the cultural significance of Notre Dame amplify the stakes of Rudy's quest. The film masterfully weaves Notre Dame into the narrative, elevating Rudy's journey beyond a personal triumph to a collective victory for the underdogs.

Embracing Sports Clichés:

Reworking Clichés into Emotional Beats: "Rudy" embraces certain sports clichés, turning them into emotional beats that resonate with audiences. The film acknowledges the familiarity of the underdog narrative but uses it as a framework to explore the nuances of Rudy's personal struggle. By reworking clichés into poignant moments, the filmmakers tap into the collective emotional consciousness associated with sports dramas while infusing the story with authenticity.

The Power of the Underdog Trope: The underdog trope, far from being a narrative crutch, becomes a powerful tool for emotional engagement. Rudy's journey embodies the collective human experience of overcoming adversity, pursuing dreams, and defying the odds. The film's adherence to certain sports film conventions serves as a bridge, allowing audiences to connect with Rudy's story on a visceral level.

Musical Score and Emotional Resonance:

Jerry Goldsmith's Score: The musical score by Jerry Goldsmith plays a pivotal role in enhancing the emotional resonance of "Rudy." Goldsmith's composition captures the highs and lows of Rudy's journey, punctuating key moments with a stirring musical backdrop. The score becomes an integral part of the film's emotional language, complementing the visuals and performances to evoke a powerful response from the audience.

The Use of Motivational Themes: Motivational themes within the score contribute to the film's inspirational tone. The music becomes a narrative force that propels Rudy forward, conveying the character's determination and indomitable spirit. The emotional synergy between the score and the storytelling elevates the viewing experience, making "Rudy" not just a sports drama but a symphony of human triumph.

Rudy's Legacy and Lasting Impact:

Enduring Inspirational Symbol: "Rudy" endures as an inspirational symbol that extends beyond the confines of sports cinema. Rudy Ruettiger's story has become synonymous with perseverance, reminding individuals that passion and determination can transcend circumstances. The film's ability to inspire, motivate, and resonate with audiences has solidified its place in the pantheon of cinematic tales of triumph.

Influence on Sports Films: The impact of "Rudy" reverberates in the realm of sports films, influencing subsequent narratives that seek to capture the spirit of underdog stories. The film's enduring popularity has contributed to a cultural appreciation for stories that celebrate the human spirit's triumph over adversity.

Conclusion: A Cinematic Testament to Perseverance:

In conclusion, "Rudy" stands as a cinematic testament to the power of perseverance and the indomitable spirit that propels individuals to defy the odds. By bringing Rudy Ruettiger's inspirational journey to the big screen, the filmmakers crafted a narrative that transcends sports fandom, resonating with audiences on a deeply human level. Through the creative synergy of storytelling, performances, and visual aesthetics, "Rudy" not only captures the essence of an underdog's triumph but cements its place as a timeless beacon of inspiration in the world of cinema.

## Sean Astin's Breakout Dramatic Performance

In the landscape of sports cinema, certain performances stand out as defining moments that elevate a film from a mere retelling of events to a deeply resonant and emotive experience. In the case of "Rudy" (1993), Sean Astin's portrayal of Daniel "Rudy" Ruettiger is nothing short of a breakout dramatic performance. Astin, known for his earlier roles in family-friendly films, transformed into the embodiment of determination, heart, and unwavering spirit in his portrayal of the real-life underdog who defied all odds to achieve his dream of playing college football at the University of Notre Dame. In this exploration, we delve into Sean Astin's breakout dramatic performance in "Rudy," examining the nuances of his portrayal, the emotional depth he brought to the character, and the lasting impact of his transformative role.

Introduction to Sean Astin's Career:

Early Career and Familial Legacy: Before "Rudy," Sean Astin had established himself in Hollywood, albeit in roles that were markedly different from the character-driven drama of the sports genre. His early career included notable performances in films such as "The Goonies" (1985) and "The War of the Roses" (1989). As the son of actress Patty Duke and adoptive son of actor John Astin, he carried a familial legacy into the industry.

Transition to Dramatic Roles: "Rudy" marked a significant turning point in Astin's career as he transitioned from lighter, family-oriented fare to the realm of dramatic storytelling. This shift showcased Astin's versatility as an actor, signaling to audiences and the industry alike that he was capable of delivering nuanced and emotionally charged performances.

The Role of Rudy Ruettiger:

Capturing the Essence of Rudy: Portraying a real-life figure comes with its own set of challenges, especially when that figure is as iconic as Rudy Ruettiger. Astin faced the task of not only embodying Rudy physically but also capturing the essence of his indomitable spirit. The success of the film hinged on Astin's ability to convey Rudy's journey authentically, from his humble beginnings to his triumphant moment on the football field at Notre Dame.

Emotional Arc and Character Development: Astin's breakout performance in "Rudy" is characterized by the skillful navigation of the character's emotional arc. From Rudy's early struggles and relentless pursuit of his dream to the moments of self-doubt and eventual triumph, Astin brings a depth to the character that transcends the sports drama genre. The gradual development of Rudy becomes a testament to Astin's commitment to portraying the intricacies of the human spirit.

Authenticity in Portrayal:

Physical Transformation: One of the hallmarks of Astin's performance in "Rudy" is his physical transformation to embody the titular character. Beyond mere resemblance, Astin underwent rigorous training to convincingly portray the athleticism required for the role. This commitment to physical authenticity added a layer of realism to the portrayal, allowing audiences to fully invest in the character's journey.

Embracing Rudy's Vulnerabilities: Astin's portrayal of Rudy goes beyond the archetypal underdog persona. While the film celebrates Rudy's tenacity and resilience, Astin also embraces the character's vulnerabilities. Whether facing familial expectations, academic challenges, or the skepticism of those around him, Rudy's journey is marked by moments of doubt and introspection. Astin navigates these aspects with a delicate touch, ensuring that Rudy remains a relatable and fully realized character.

The Emotional Core of the Film:

Connecting with Audiences: Sean Astin's breakout performance in "Rudy" lies in his ability to forge a deep emotional connection with audiences. Through his portrayal of Rudy, Astin taps into universal themes of perseverance, ambition, and the pursuit of dreams. Viewers see Rudy not just as a football player but as a symbol of the human spirit's capacity to overcome adversity.

Elevating the Emotional Beats: Dramatic moments within the film are elevated by Astin's nuanced performance. Whether it's the heart-wrenching rejections, the poignant interactions with his family, or the triumphant climax on the football field, Astin infuses each scene with emotional authenticity. His performance serves as the emotional anchor of the film, guiding viewers through the highs and lows of Rudy's journey.

Chemistry with Co-Stars:

Jon Favreau as D-Bob: The chemistry between Sean Astin and his co-stars contributes significantly to the film's emotional resonance. In particular, his dynamic with Jon Favreau, who plays Rudy's friend and fellow Notre Dame student D-Bob, adds a layer of authenticity to the narrative. The camaraderie between the characters, coupled with Astin and Favreau's on-screen chemistry, enhances the film's portrayal of friendship and support.

Ned Beatty and Charles S. Dutton: Astin's interactions with seasoned actors like Ned Beatty and Charles S. Dutton, who play pivotal roles in Rudy's journey, further showcase his ability to hold his own in scenes with experienced performers. The mentor-mentee dynamic between Astin and these actors adds depth to the character relationships, contributing to the overall emotional impact of the film.

Balancing Intensity and Nuance:

Intensity in Pursuit of Dreams: "Rudy" is a film marked by intensity, both in its sports sequences and in the emotional beats that define the narrative. Astin's portrayal of Rudy embodies this intensity, particularly in the scenes where Rudy confronts the formidable challenges before him. Astin channels the character's relentless drive with conviction, making each triumph and setback feel visceral and impactful.

Nuanced Moments of Reflection: Amidst the intensity, Astin brings moments of nuanced reflection to the character. Rudy's internal struggles and moments of self-discovery are conveyed with subtlety, allowing Astin to showcase the range of emotions that define the human experience. These nuanced moments add layers to Rudy's character, making him more than a one-dimensional underdog.

Impact of Sean Astin's Performance:

Cultural Icon of Perseverance: Sean Astin's portrayal of Rudy has transformed the character into a cultural icon of perseverance. The image of Astin, clad in a Notre Dame jersey, encapsulates the spirit of overcoming odds and pursuing one's dreams. Rudy's journey, as brought to life by Astin, has transcended the confines of the film to become a symbol of inspiration for audiences worldwide.

Legacy in Sports Cinema: Astin's breakout performance in "Rudy" has left an enduring legacy in the realm of sports cinema. The film, and by extension, Astin's portrayal of Rudy, has become a touchstone for stories of underdogs defying expectations. Subsequent sports films have looked to "Rudy" as a benchmark for capturing the emotional core of real-life narratives.

Conclusion: Sean Astin's Artistry and Rudy's Timeless Resonance:

In conclusion, Sean Astin's breakout dramatic performance in "Rudy" stands as a testament to his artistry as an actor and the enduring resonance of Rudy Ruettiger's story. Astin's ability to authentically portray the complexities of the human spirit, coupled with his physical commitment to the role, elevates "Rudy" beyond a sports drama to a timeless exploration of determination, heart, and the pursuit of dreams. Through Astin's transformative portrayal, Rudy's journey becomes a universal tale that continues to inspire and uplift audiences, solidifying its place in the annals of cinematic storytelling.

## The Appeal of the Ultimate Underdog Tale

In the vast landscape of sports cinema, few narratives resonate as profoundly as the tale of the underdog—a figure defying the odds, overcoming adversity, and achieving against all expectations. "Rudy" (1993), directed by David Anspaugh, stands as a quintessential example of the ultimate underdog tale, weaving a narrative that transcends the football field to become a symbol of perseverance, passion, and the indomitable human spirit. In this exploration, we delve into the elements that contribute to the enduring appeal of "Rudy" as the ultimate underdog tale, examining the storytelling techniques, character dynamics, and thematic richness that elevate the film to a timeless and universally resonant story.

Introduction to the Underdog Archetype:

Universal Allure of the Underdog: The underdog archetype has captivated audiences across cultures and generations, tapping into a primal human fascination with stories of triumph against adversity. Whether in sports, literature, or cinema, the underdog narrative resonates because it speaks to the fundamental human desire for victory over challenges, for the triumph of the human spirit.

Identification and Empathy: At the core of the underdog tale's appeal is its ability to evoke identification and empathy. Viewers see reflections of their own struggles, dreams, and aspirations in the underdog's journey. The underdog becomes a surrogate for the audience, embodying the collective yearning for success against overwhelming odds.

Rudy Ruettiger: A Relatable Everyman:

Humble Beginnings and Relatable Struggles: Rudy Ruettiger's journey epitomizes the relatable underdog narrative. Born into a working-class family in Joliet, Illinois, Rudy faced financial constraints, academic challenges, and the skepticism of those around him. His story begins not on a grand stage but in the everyday struggles of an individual striving for something beyond the ordinary.

Dreams Beyond Conventional Success: Unlike traditional sports narratives that often focus on superstar athletes, Rudy's dreams extend beyond the pursuit of conventional success. His goal of playing football for the University of Notre Dame reflects a deeply personal and symbolic quest—an aspiration fueled by passion and a desire to prove that even those with modest backgrounds can achieve extraordinary feats.

David vs. Goliath:

Symbolic Significance of Notre Dame: The choice of Notre Dame as the backdrop for Rudy's journey adds a layer of symbolic significance to the David vs. Goliath narrative. Notre Dame, with its storied football tradition and cultural prominence, becomes the Goliath against which Rudy, the ultimate David, strives. The university's iconic status amplifies the scale of Rudy's underdog quest, turning a personal aspiration into a collective symbol of triumph over giants.

Subverting Sports Tropes: "Rudy" subverts traditional sports film tropes by focusing on an individual whose talents may not align with the athletic prowess typically associated with football heroes. Rudy's journey challenges the notion that success in sports is solely defined by physical prowess, highlighting the importance of heart, determination, and unwavering belief in oneself.

Underdog Dynamics in the Narrative:

Setbacks and Rejections: The underdog narrative is characterized by setbacks and rejections that test the protagonist's resolve. Rudy faces numerous obstacles, from academic struggles to the skepticism of his peers and family. These challenges become crucibles that forge his determination, creating a narrative tension that propels the story forward.

Mentors and Allies: Integral to the underdog tale are mentors and allies who recognize the protagonist's potential and offer support. Rudy's interactions with figures like Father Cavanaugh, Fortune, and Coach Ara Parseghian provide emotional anchor points in the narrative. The relationships underscore the importance of communal support in overcoming adversity.

Building Emotional Investment:

Relational Depth: The emotional investment in an underdog tale is often built on relational depth. Rudy's relationships with his family, friends, and mentors are integral to the film's emotional resonance. The audience becomes invested not only in Rudy's personal journey but in the collective web of connections that sustain and inspire him.

Family Dynamics: The portrayal of Rudy's family dynamics adds emotional weight to the narrative. The financial struggles and the expectations placed on Rudy by his working-class family create a backdrop against which his dreams unfold. The film navigates the complexities of familial support and expectations, making Rudy's journey a reflection of broader familial dynamics.

Cinematic Techniques and Symbolism:

Montage Sequences and Symbolic Imagery: Cinematic techniques play a crucial role in enhancing the emotional impact of Rudy's underdog journey. Montage sequences, coupled with symbolic imagery, create a visual language that communicates the passage of time, the evolution of Rudy's character, and the milestones of his quest. The use of Notre Dame's iconic landmarks and football rituals adds layers of symbolism to the narrative.

Musical Score: Jerry Goldsmith's musical score contributes significantly to the film's emotional resonance. The score, marked by motivational themes and stirring orchestrations, becomes a narrative force that elevates key moments in Rudy's journey. The synergy between visual storytelling and musical accompaniment creates a powerful emotional experience for the audience.

Struggles and Sacrifices:

Academic Challenges: The underdog narrative often incorporates academic challenges as a subplot. In Rudy's case, his struggles with academics become a tangible representation of the obstacles he faces. The film navigates the tension between Rudy's passion for football and the practical challenges of meeting academic standards, adding a layer of realism to the narrative.

Sacrifices for the Dream: The ultimate underdog tale involves sacrifices, and Rudy's journey is no exception. From working at the Notre Dame stadium to prove his commitment to enduring physical hardships during practices, Rudy's sacrifices become markers of his dedication to the dream. These sacrifices resonate with audiences, reinforcing the idea that triumph often comes at a personal cost.

Climactic Triumph and Catharsis:

The Notre Dame Game: The climactic triumph in an underdog tale is a pivotal moment that serves as catharsis for the audience. Rudy's inclusion in the Notre Dame football game becomes the culmination of years of struggle, rejection, and unwavering persistence. The game is not just a sports spectacle; it is a symbolic victory for every individual who has dared to dream against formidable odds.

Emotional Release: The emotional release experienced by the audience during the climactic triumph is a testament to the narrative's ability to evoke empathy and resonance. The underdog's victory becomes a shared victory, resonating with viewers who have faced their own challenges and setbacks. The emotional release serves as a cathartic celebration of human resilience.

Legacy of the Underdog Tale:

Enduring Inspiration: The enduring appeal of the ultimate underdog tale lies in its ability to inspire across generations. "Rudy" continues to be a source of inspiration for individuals facing challenges, setbacks, or pursuing dreams that may seem unattainable. The film's legacy extends beyond the screen, becoming a cultural touchstone for stories of triumph and perseverance.

Cinematic Influence: "Rudy" has had a lasting impact on the cinematic landscape, influencing subsequent sports films and underdog narratives. Filmmakers and storytellers look to "Rudy" as a benchmark for capturing the emotional core of real-life stories, recognizing its ability to resonate with audiences on a deeply human level.

Conclusion: Rudy as the Embodiment of Human Triumph:

In conclusion, "Rudy" stands as the embodiment of the ultimate underdog tale—a narrative that transcends the football field to become a timeless exploration of human triumph. The film's enduring appeal lies in its ability to tap into universal themes of perseverance, passion, and the indomitable human spirit. Rudy Ruettiger's journey, authentically portrayed on screen, resonates as a symbol of inspiration, reminding audiences that even in the face of seemingly insurmountable odds, the human spirit can soar to remarkable heights. As the ultimate underdog, Rudy becomes not just a character in a film but a testament to the resilience and determination that define the human experience.

### Questioning the Truth Behind the Legend

In the realm of biographical films, the delicate interplay between truth and fiction often shapes the narrative, inviting audiences to question the extent to which cinematic portrayals align with historical realities. "Rudy" (1993), directed by David Anspaugh, presents the inspirational story of Rudy Ruettiger's journey from a working-class background to achieving his dream of playing football for the University of Notre Dame. However, the film, like many based on true stories, navigates the fine line between depicting actual events and employing cinematic liberties for dramatic effect. In this exploration, we delve into the complexities of "Rudy" as a biographical film, questioning the truth behind the legend and examining how creative decisions, narrative choices, and the portrayal of characters contribute to the construction of a cinematic narrative that transcends mere factual accuracy.

Introduction: Balancing Fact and Fiction:

Cinematic Interpretation of Reality: The genre of biographical filmmaking inherently involves a level of interpretation and selective storytelling. "Rudy," while grounded in the real-life experiences of Rudy Ruettiger, embraces a cinematic interpretation that goes beyond a mere retelling of facts. The film's narrative choices invite viewers to engage with the emotional core of Rudy's journey rather than a strict adherence to historical accuracy.

The Power of Myth: In constructing a legend, filmmakers often rely on mythic elements that amplify the emotional resonance of the narrative. Rudy Ruettiger's story, while grounded in his actual achievements, takes on mythic proportions in the film. This myth-making process, driven by the desire to create a universally resonant underdog tale, prompts viewers to question where historical truth ends and the mythic narrative begins.

Creative License in Rudy's Journey:

Compression of Timelines: One of the common creative liberties taken in biographical films is the compression of timelines. "Rudy" condenses events and experiences into a narrative that unfolds seamlessly within the constraints of a feature-length film. This compression serves the dual purpose of maintaining pacing and heightening the emotional impact, but it raises questions about the chronological accuracy of events.

Composite Characters: To streamline complex narratives, biographical films often introduce composite characters—individuals who represent a confluence of real-life figures. "Rudy" employs this technique, blending characters and experiences to create a cohesive and emotionally resonant story. However, this blending blurs the line between specific historical details and fictional amalgamations.

The Legend of Rudy Ruettiger:

From Reality to Symbol: As "Rudy" transforms the real-life Rudy Ruettiger into a cinematic symbol of determination and triumph, the line between the individual and the archetype blurs. The legend of Rudy transcends the specifics of his journey, becoming a cultural touchstone for anyone striving against adversity. The film's emphasis on the symbolic power of

Rudy's story invites viewers to consider the broader implications of his narrative rather than its factual accuracy.

The Influence of Notre Dame: Notre Dame, with its iconic status in American collegiate sports, plays a central role in elevating Rudy's legend. The university becomes a character in itself, symbolizing not only a prestigious institution but also the embodiment of Rudy's aspirations. The film's portrayal of Notre Dame contributes to the mythic quality of Rudy's journey, emphasizing the transformative power of dreams against the backdrop of an esteemed institution.

Narrative Choices and Character Portrayals:

Emotional Authenticity vs. Factual Precision: Biographical films often grapple with the tension between emotional authenticity and factual precision. "Rudy" prioritizes the former, weaving a narrative that resonates emotionally with audiences. While certain details may be altered for dramatic effect, the film's commitment to capturing the essence of Rudy's spirit allows viewers to connect with the emotional core of his journey.

Father Cavanaugh as Mentor Figure: The character of Father Cavanaugh serves as a mentor figure in Rudy's journey, providing guidance and support. While based on real individuals who influenced Rudy, the film consolidates these influences into a single character. Father Cavanaugh becomes a narrative anchor, representing the wisdom and encouragement that propel Rudy forward. This choice, though not strictly factual, enhances the film's thematic resonance.

Rudy's Motivations and Personal Growth:

Balancing Realism with Cinematic Drama: In exploring Rudy's motivations, the film strikes a balance between realism and cinematic drama. The portrayal of Rudy's desire to honor his family and overcome personal challenges resonates emotionally, even if certain details are heightened for dramatic effect. The film's commitment to capturing the emotional truth of Rudy's motivations allows audiences to empathize with his journey.

Personal Growth as Cinematic Arc: Rudy's personal growth throughout the film follows a classic cinematic arc. From the early struggles and rejections to the climactic triumph, the narrative constructs a trajectory of growth and self-discovery. While this arc aligns with Rudy's real-life experiences, the film's emphasis on a structured narrative arc reinforces the cinematic storytelling conventions that shape biographical dramas.

Questioning Historical Accuracy:

Public Reception vs. Historical Verification: The public reception of a biographical film often influences the perception of historical accuracy. While "Rudy" garnered widespread acclaim for its inspirational narrative, questions arise about the extent to which the film adheres to the verified details of Rudy Ruettiger's life. The dichotomy between public perception and historical verification underscores the complexities of presenting true stories on screen.

Real-Life Achievements vs. Cinematic Symbolism: Rudy Ruettiger's real-life achievements are indisputable, yet the film's cinematic symbolism transcends specific events. The climactic football game at Notre Dame, while based on actual circumstances, takes on a mythic quality that goes beyond the particulars of the game itself. The film's emphasis on cinematic symbolism prompts viewers to consider the broader implications of Rudy's story.

Authenticity in Cinematic Storytelling:

Truth in Emotional Resonance: While certain details may be subject to creative interpretation, the emotional truth embedded in "Rudy" remains a potent force. The film's ability to resonate emotionally, to capture the essence of Rudy's journey, and to evoke universal themes of perseverance and triumph speaks to the authenticity of cinematic storytelling. In questioning the truth behind the legend, the focus shifts from factual minutiae to the enduring impact of the narrative.

The Cinematic Rudy vs. the Historical Rudy: Viewers are presented with the cinematic Rudy—an amalgamation of historical events, emotional truths, and symbolic resonance. The cinematic representation becomes a lens through which audiences engage with the broader themes of the underdog narrative. The distinction between the cinematic Rudy and the historical Rudy invites contemplation on the nature of storytelling and its role in shaping cultural myths.

Conclusion: The Enduring Paradox of Cinematic Biographies:

In conclusion, "Rudy" encapsulates the enduring paradox inherent in cinematic biographies—the tension between historical accuracy and the power of storytelling. The film navigates this tension by prioritizing emotional authenticity, inviting viewers to connect with the spirit of Rudy's journey rather than scrutinize the minutiae of factual details. As Rudy's legend transcends the boundaries of his real-life achievements, the film becomes a testament to the enduring power of cinematic narratives to inspire, uplift, and question the very nature of truth in storytelling. In the end, the legend of Rudy Ruettiger, as presented on screen, invites audiences to ponder not just the historical facts but the timeless themes of resilience, dreams, and the indomitable human spirit that define the ultimate underdog tale.

## Chapter 5: The Replacements (2000)
## Capitalizing on the 1987 Players' Strike

In the annals of sports cinema, few films capture the essence of the tumultuous relationship between athletes and team management as vividly as "The Replacements" (2000). Directed by Howard Deutch, this gridiron comedy takes center stage against the backdrop of the 1987 NFL Players' Strike—a pivotal moment in the league's history. The film unfolds a narrative where replacement players, a motley crew of misfits and unconventional athletes, step into the limelight when professional football grinds to a halt due to labor disputes. In this exploration, we delve into how "The Replacements" strategically capitalizes on the real-life 1987 players' strike, examining the film's narrative choices, character dynamics, and the resonant themes that emerge from the collision of sports, labor, and the human spirit.

Introduction: Contextualizing the Players' Strike

Historical Significance of the 1987 Strike: The 1987 NFL Players' Strike stands as a watershed moment in professional football, marking the first work stoppage in the league's history. Players, dissatisfied with the terms of their collective bargaining agreement, opted to withhold their services, creating a void in the football landscape. "The Replacements" seizes upon this historical juncture, transforming it into a canvas for a comedic yet poignant exploration of the resilience of the human spirit in the face of adversity.

Impact on Regular Season: The strike had tangible consequences on the regular season, with teams fielding replacement players during the absence of their regular rosters. The film captures the unique circumstances that arose from this situation, highlighting the challenges, controversies, and unexpected moments that unfolded on and off the field. By leveraging this historical backdrop, "The Replacements" infuses its narrative with a blend of satire, sportsmanship, and the universal theme of the underdog.

Setting the Stage: Labor Disputes and Team Dynamics

Labor Strife and Team Dysfunction: The film unfolds against the canvas of labor strife, portraying the strained relationship between players and team management. The dichotomy between the striking professional players and the replacement athletes becomes a microcosm of larger issues related to labor negotiations, athlete agency, and the dynamics of power within professional sports. "The Replacements" weaves a narrative that delves beyond the gridiron, exploring the complexities of labor relations that reverberate through the world of professional football.

The Impact on Team Dynamics: With the regular players on strike, teams were forced to recruit replacement players hastily. "The Replacements" captures the ensuing chaos, as team dynamics are upended, and coaches grapple with the challenge of melding a disparate group of individuals into a cohesive unit. The film adeptly explores the clash of egos, athletic backgrounds, and personalities within the replacement team, providing a humorous yet insightful commentary on the delicate balance required in assembling a functional football squad.

Characterizing the Replacement Players: A Diverse Ensemble

Archetypes and Stereotypes: "The Replacements" introduces audiences to a cast of characters that embody various archetypes and stereotypes associated with sports. From the former college quarterback seeking redemption to the convict with a penchant for violence, each replacement player represents a distinct facet of the broader sports narrative. The film uses these archetypes strategically to navigate themes of redemption, second chances, and the universality of the human desire for athletic achievement.

Falco's Redemption Arc: At the heart of the film is Shane Falco, played by Keanu Reeves, a former college football star whose career took a downward spiral. His narrative arc encapsulates the theme of redemption—a once-promising athlete seeking a second chance to prove his worth. As the de facto leader of the replacement team, Falco's journey becomes a focal point for exploring the transformative power of sports in providing individuals with an opportunity for redemption and personal growth.

Navigating Comedy and Heartfelt Moments

Satirical Elements: "The Replacements" infuses humor into its narrative by embracing satirical elements that poke fun at both the eccentricities of replacement players and the conventions of professional football. The film revels in the absurdity of the situation—untrained athletes, unconventional strategies, and the clash between traditional football norms and the unorthodox methods employed by the replacements. This comedic lens serves as a vehicle for commentary on the idiosyncrasies of sports culture.

Heartfelt Moments Amidst the Comedy: Beneath the comedic veneer, the film strategically interweaves heartfelt moments that resonate with audiences on a deeper level. Whether exploring the camaraderie among replacement players, Falco's personal journey, or the unexpected triumphs on the field, "The Replacements" manages to balance its comedic tone with poignant reflections on the human condition. This tonal dexterity allows the film to transcend mere satire, offering viewers a narrative that is both entertaining and emotionally resonant.

On-Field Drama and Cinematic Spectacle

Game Sequences: "The Replacements" leverages the inherent drama of football games to propel its narrative forward. The film's depiction of on-field action, marked by unconventional plays, unorthodox strategies, and the sheer unpredictability of the replacements' athletic abilities, creates a cinematic spectacle that captures the essence of sports entertainment. Through dynamic game sequences, the film taps into the adrenaline-fueled excitement of football, emphasizing the joy of competition and the thrill of the unexpected.

Confrontations and Triumphs: Key moments in the film revolve around the confrontations between the replacements and the more established professional players who cross the picket line. These showdowns become symbolic clashes between different ideologies—loyalty to the team, solidarity among players, and the pursuit of personal ambitions. The triumphs of the replacements in these confrontations elevate the film beyond a simple sports comedy, transforming it into a narrative that explores themes of resilience, defiance, and the pursuit of dreams against formidable odds.

The Love Story and Personal Stakes

Romantic Subplot: "The Replacements" introduces a romantic subplot between Falco and Annabelle Farrell, the team's head cheerleader played by Brooke Langton. This narrative thread adds a layer of personal stakes for the protagonist, offering a counterpoint to the larger themes of labor disputes and sportsmanship. The love story becomes a catalyst for Falco's self-discovery and emotional growth, contributing to the film's multifaceted exploration of the human experience.

Personal Stakes and Player Motivations: Each replacement player brings a unique set of personal stakes and motivations to the field. Whether driven by the pursuit of a second chance, financial incentives, or the sheer love of the game, these individual motivations contribute to the film's thematic richness. "The Replacements" deftly navigates the intersection of personal and collective stakes, presenting a nuanced portrait of athletes driven by a variety of aspirations.

Reflections on Labor and Athlete Agency

Labor Struggles as Background Commentary: While "The Replacements" uses the 1987 players' strike as a backdrop for its narrative, the film does not delve deeply into the intricacies of labor negotiations or the broader socioeconomic context of the strike. Instead, it uses the strike as a vehicle for exploring broader themes of defiance, camaraderie, and the resilience of the human spirit. The labor struggles serve as a contextual backdrop that adds weight to the on-field drama and personal journeys of the characters.

Athlete Agency and Individual Choices: The replacement players in the film are faced with a choice—cross the picket line and play as replacements or stand in solidarity with their striking counterparts. This exploration of athlete agency becomes a central theme, prompting viewers to consider the complexities of individual choices within the broader framework of labor disputes. "The Replacements" offers a commentary on the autonomy of athletes to navigate their careers and make decisions that align with their personal aspirations.

Cultural Commentary and Reception

Pop Culture References: "The Replacements" integrates pop culture references and nods to the zeitgeist of the late 1990s. From the soundtrack featuring iconic songs of the era to the inclusion of cultural touchstones, the film positions itself within a specific cultural milieu. These references contribute to the film's appeal, connecting with audiences through a shared cultural lexicon and establishing a sense of nostalgia for the period in which it was produced.

Reception and Cultural Impact: Upon its release, "The Replacements" received a mix of critical reviews and moderate box office success. While some critics praised its humor and energetic performances, others found fault in its formulaic approach to sports comedies. Over time, however, the film has garnered a dedicated fan base and achieved a level of cultural impact, especially among those who appreciate its blend of sports, comedy, and underdog narratives.

Conclusion: "The Replacements" as a Cultural Intersection

In conclusion, "The Replacements" occupies a unique space within the realm of sports cinema, leveraging the historical context of the 1987 NFL Players' Strike to craft a narrative that transcends the boundaries of traditional sports comedies. The film strategically capitalizes on the labor disputes of the time, using them as a springboard to explore themes of resilience, individual agency, and the triumph of the human spirit. By infusing its narrative with a diverse ensemble of characters, a balance of humor and heartfelt moments, and dynamic on-field action, "The Replacements" creates a cultural intersection where sports, labor, and personal aspirations converge. As the replacements defy expectations and forge a collective identity on the football field, the film invites viewers to reflect on the timeless themes of camaraderie, defiance, and the enduring appeal of the underdog narrative in the ever-evolving landscape of sports and cinema.

## Building a Comedic Story Around Replacement Players

In the landscape of sports cinema, "The Replacements" (2000) stands out as a comedic gem that not only embraces the excitement of football but also weaves humor into the fabric of its narrative. Directed by Howard Deutch, the film ventures into the uncharted territory of replacement players, a motley crew of athletes stepping into the shoes of their striking counterparts during the 1987 NFL Players' Strike. In this exploration, we delve into the art of building a comedic story around replacement players, examining the film's unique blend of humor, character dynamics, and the inventive ways in which it navigates the collision of sports and comedy.

Introduction: Crafting Comedy on the Gridiron

Humor in Sports Cinema: While sports films often gravitate towards drama, triumph, and the emotional highs and lows of athletic competition, "The Replacements" takes a daring detour into the realm of comedy. By choosing replacement players as its focal point, the film not only explores the challenges and absurdities of professional football but also infuses the narrative with humor that resonates both with sports enthusiasts and casual viewers. This chapter unravels the intricacies of building a comedic narrative within the framework of sports, using replacement players as the comedic catalyst.

The 1987 NFL Players' Strike: At the heart of the humor in "The Replacements" lies the historical context of the 1987 NFL Players' Strike. The strike created a void in the football landscape, paving the way for replacement players to take center stage. The film cleverly capitalizes on this real-life situation, using it as a launching pad for comedic scenarios, unconventional team dynamics, and unexpected moments that form the backbone of its humor.

Setting the Stage: Introduction of the Replacement Players

Character Introductions: "The Replacements" introduces audiences to a diverse ensemble of replacement players, each with their quirks, backgrounds, and unconventional skills. From the former sumo wrestler to the Welsh soccer player, the film revels in the eccentricity of its characters. The humor emerges not only from their lack of professional football experience but also from the clash of personalities and athletic backgrounds, setting the stage for comedic interactions on and off the field.

Shane Falco as the Reluctant Leader: Central to the comedic ensemble is Shane Falco, played by Keanu Reeves. As the former college football star turned disillusioned nobody, Falco becomes the reluctant leader of the replacement team. His journey, infused with comedic undertones, serves as a narrative anchor, providing both humor and emotional depth to the film. The juxtaposition of Falco's charisma and the eclectic mix of replacement players amplifies the comedic potential of their interactions.

Humor in Team Dynamics: The Art of the Ensemble Cast

Eccentric Archetypes and Stereotypes: "The Replacements" leans into the use of archetypes and stereotypes, transforming them into comedic gold. Each replacement player represents a distinct stereotype or archetype associated with sports, allowing the film to playfully subvert expectations. Whether it's the "Nigel with the one 'L'" kicker or the convict with a penchant for violence, the film cleverly exploits these comedic tropes to generate laughter while exploring the universality of the human desire for athletic achievement.

Conflict and Camaraderie: The humor in team dynamics arises from the clash of egos, the unconventional skills of individual players, and the challenges of forging camaraderie among a disparate group. The film navigates conflicts with comedic finesse, turning disagreements into punchlines and transforming the tensions within the team into moments of levity. The delicate balance between conflict and camaraderie becomes a comedic tightrope that "The Replacements" skillfully walks.

On-Field Comedy: Unconventional Plays and Strategies

Unorthodox Training Montage: Comedy extends onto the field as the replacement players engage in a training montage that eschews traditional sports training tropes. From sumo wrestling drills to the unique preparation methods of the Welsh soccer player, the film mines humor from the unconventional training methods employed by the replacements. This comedic approach not only serves as a departure from typical sports training sequences but also reinforces the film's commitment to subverting sports movie conventions.

Inventive Playbook: "The Replacements" introduces an inventive playbook that incorporates unorthodox plays and strategies. The film uses these comedic plays to showcase the replacements' unconventional skills, turning the football field into a stage for physical comedy. Whether it's the "Ole!" play or the "Annexation of Puerto Rico," each play becomes a comedic set piece, eliciting laughter while highlighting the replacements' unscripted approach to the game.

Individual Quirks and Running Gags:

Sumo Wrestler's Dance: The film establishes running gags that punctuate the comedic rhythm of the narrative. The sumo wrestler's dance, a recurring motif, becomes both a humorous spectacle and a symbol of the replacements' unapologetic embrace of individual quirks. This running gag serves as a touchstone for the film's commitment to physical comedy and the celebration of the replacements' unconventional journey.

Earl Wilkinson's Sweet Tooth: Earl Wilkinson's affinity for candy becomes another running gag, injecting humor into tense moments and offering a recurring source of comedic relief. The film uses Earl's sweet tooth not only for laughs but also as a character trait that adds depth to his personality. These running gags contribute to the film's comedic consistency and provide a through line that connects various scenes.

The Love Story as a Comedic Element

Romantic Comedy Elements: "The Replacements" incorporates romantic comedy elements into its narrative, adding another layer of humor to the film. The budding romance between Shane Falco and Annabelle Farrell, the head cheerleader, becomes a source of comedic tension and levity. The film navigates the tropes of romantic comedy with a playful touch, infusing humor into the dynamics between the central characters.

Comedic Tensions and Resolutions: The romantic subplot becomes a vehicle for exploring comedic tensions and resolutions. From awkward interactions to humorous misunderstandings, the film uses the romantic dynamic between Falco and Annabelle to generate laughs while providing a counterpoint to the broader themes of labor disputes and sportsmanship. The comedic treatment of the love story adds a layer of lightheartedness to the film's overall tone.

Reflections on the 1987 Players' Strike: Satire and Social Commentary

Satirical Elements: While "The Replacements" primarily embraces comedy, it also incorporates satirical elements that offer a tongue-in-cheek commentary on professional football and labor disputes. The film satirizes the corporate nature of sports ownership, the performative aspects of sportsmanship, and the inherent contradictions within the world of professional football. This satirical lens allows the film to engage with broader social and cultural themes while maintaining its comedic core.

Sports as Theater: The film positions sports as a form of theater, emphasizing the performative nature of professional football. This theme is explored through comedic sequences, theatrical celebrations, and the juxtaposition of the replacements' unscripted approach with the scripted precision of the regular players. By framing sports as a theatrical spectacle, "The Replacements" invites viewers to consider the theatricality embedded within the sports industry.

Cultural Impact and Enduring Laughter

Cultural Resonance: "The Replacements" has achieved a level of cultural resonance, particularly among audiences who appreciate its unique blend of sports and comedy. The film's enduring popularity is rooted in its ability to elicit laughter through a combination of physical comedy, witty dialogue, and the charismatic performances of its ensemble cast. The cultural impact of "The Replacements" extends beyond its initial release, finding a place in the pantheon of sports comedies that continue to entertain new generations of viewers.

Legacy of Laughter: As a sports comedy, "The Replacements" leaves a legacy of laughter, remembered for its memorable characters, comedic set pieces, and the audacious premise of building a story around replacement players. The film's enduring appeal lies not only in its humor but also in its ability to infuse laughter into the world of professional football, presenting a comedic lens through which audiences can engage with the beloved spectacle of the gridiron.

Conclusion: "The Replacements" as a Comedy Touchdown

In conclusion, "The Replacements" scores a comedy touchdown by masterfully building a narrative around replacement players. The film's success in crafting humor on the gridiron stems from its inventive use of character dynamics, on-field comedy, and the integration of romantic comedy elements. By embracing the absurdity of the 1987 NFL Players' Strike and the unscripted journey of the replacements, the film creates a comedic spectacle that resonates with both sports enthusiasts and comedy aficionados. As "The Replacements" continues to elicit laughter and entertain audiences, it stands as a testament to the enduring power of humor in sports cinema and the joyous celebration of the unconventional journey of the underdog.

## Keanu Reeves as the Ragtag Team's Leader

In the vibrant tapestry of sports cinema, certain performances become iconic, leaving an indelible mark on the collective memory of audiences. In "The Replacements" (2000), Keanu Reeves takes on the role of Shane Falco, the reluctant leader of a ragtag team of replacement players thrust into the spotlight during the 1987 NFL Players' Strike. This chapter delves into the nuanced portrayal of Falco by Reeves, exploring the character's journey, the dynamics of leadership within the film, and the enduring impact of Keanu Reeves as the charismatic linchpin holding together a team of misfits.

Introduction: The Charismatic Core of the Team

Shane Falco's Resonance: At the heart of "The Replacements" lies Shane Falco, a character who transcends the boundaries of traditional sports movie protagonists. Portrayed by Keanu Reeves, Falco becomes the charismatic core around which the ragtag team of replacement players coalesces. This chapter examines how Reeves infuses Falco with a unique blend of vulnerability, charisma, and determination, elevating the character to a status of enduring resonance within the annals of sports cinema.

The Reluctant Leader: Shane Falco's Journey

Introduction to Shane Falco: Shane Falco emerges from the shadows of his own unfulfilled potential, a former college football star whose dreams were deferred by personal setbacks. Reeves introduces audiences to a character whose journey unfolds as a synthesis of redemption, self-discovery, and leadership. The film strategically positions Falco as the reluctant leader, a figure whose journey becomes a metaphor for the broader themes of second chances and the indomitable human spirit.

Vulnerability and Depth: Reeves infuses Falco with a vulnerability that sets him apart from traditional sports movie heroes. Falco's flaws, insecurities, and the scars of past failures become integral components of his character. Reeves navigates this vulnerability with nuance, allowing audiences to empathize with Falco's internal struggles while rooting for his external triumphs. This portrayal adds depth to the character, transforming him into a three-dimensional protagonist whose journey resonates on an emotional level.

Charismatic Presence: Keanu Reeves as Shane Falco

Reeves's Unique Charisma: Keanu Reeves brings a distinctive brand of charisma to the character of Shane Falco. Known for his understated yet compelling on-screen presence, Reeves infuses Falco with a quiet confidence that draws viewers in. The actor's ability to convey emotion through subtle expressions and nuanced delivery contributes to the authenticity of Falco's character, making him a relatable and compelling figure within the narrative.

Balancing Humor and Pathos: "The Replacements" navigates a delicate balance between humor and pathos, and Reeves plays a pivotal role in maintaining this equilibrium. Falco's interactions with his fellow replacement players, the comedic moments on the field, and the more poignant scenes of self-reflection all benefit from Reeves's ability to seamlessly transition between humor and genuine emotion. This balance elevates the film beyond a simple sports comedy, turning it into a character-driven narrative with a charismatic leader at its helm.

Navigating Relationships: Falco and the Ragtag Team

Dynamic with Teammates: Reeves's portrayal of Falco establishes a dynamic with his teammates that goes beyond the conventional tropes of sports movie camaraderie. Falco's interactions with the diverse ensemble of replacement players become a focal point for both humor and character development. Reeves navigates the comedic nuances of these relationships with a natural ease, allowing Falco to connect with each teammate in a way that contributes to the film's overall comedic and emotional resonance.

Romantic Dynamic: The romantic subplot between Falco and Annabelle Farrell, played by Brooke Langton, adds another layer to Reeves's performance. The chemistry between Reeves and Langton is palpable, and Reeves infuses the romantic dynamic with a blend of charm and vulnerability. The romantic subplot becomes a vehicle for exploring Falco's personal growth and emotional depth, further showcasing Reeves's ability to navigate the complexities of character relationships.

Leadership Dynamics: Falco as the Team Captain

The Reluctant Captain: Falco's journey to becoming the team captain is marked by reluctance and self-doubt. Reeves conveys the internal conflict within Falco, who initially resists assuming a leadership role due to the weight of his past failures. This reluctance becomes a source of both humor and genuine character development, as Falco transforms from a hesitant figure into a captain who leads with a unique blend of authenticity and determination.

Leading by Example: Reeves embodies the principle of leading by example, a central tenet of Falco's leadership style. Whether it's diving into the mud during a practice session or rallying the team during moments of adversity, Falco's leadership is rooted in action rather than rhetoric. Reeves's physical commitment to the role enhances the authenticity of Falco's leadership, reinforcing the idea that true leadership is earned through deeds rather than words.

The Journey of Redemption: Falco's Arc

Redemption Through Football: At its core, "The Replacements" is a story of redemption, and Reeves navigates Falco's redemption arc with a nuanced touch. The football field becomes the crucible through which Falco confronts his past and seeks redemption for his perceived failures. Reeves's portrayal captures the emotional stakes of Falco's journey, transforming the gridiron into a stage for personal triumph and growth.

Questioning the Legend: As the film progresses, Falco's journey prompts viewers to question the nature of legends and heroism. Reeves introduces an element of self-awareness to Falco, a character who questions the grandeur bestowed upon athletes and grapples with the disparity between perception and reality. This introspective layer adds complexity to Falco's character, challenging traditional sports movie tropes and offering a fresh perspective on the nature of heroism.

Dynamic with Coach McGinty: Gene Hackman and Keanu Reeves

Chemistry with Gene Hackman: "The Replacements" benefits not only from Reeves's performance but also from the dynamic between him and Gene Hackman, who plays Coach Jimmy McGinty. The chemistry between the two actors adds depth to the mentor-protégé relationship between Falco and McGinty. Reeves's ability to hold his own alongside a seasoned actor like Hackman contributes to the film's overall narrative strength.

Conveying Respect and Growth: Reeves conveys a palpable sense of respect for Hackman's character, and this dynamic becomes a vessel for Falco's growth. The mentorship dynamic allows Reeves to explore different facets of Falco's character, from the initial skepticism towards authority to the eventual recognition of the value of guidance and mentorship. The scenes between Reeves and Hackman showcase the actor's ability to convey a range of emotions, from defiance to humility.

Balancing Act: Falco's Comedic and Emotional Beats

Humor Amidst Adversity: Reeves's performance in "The Replacements" shines in its ability to inject humor into moments of adversity. Whether it's navigating the eccentricities of his teammates, confronting his own insecurities, or facing off against professional players, Reeves infuses Falco with a comedic sensibility that resonates with audiences. The actor's timing and delivery contribute to the film's overall comedic rhythm, turning potential moments of tension into opportunities for laughter.

Emotional Resonance: Amidst the humor, Reeves also brings emotional resonance to Falco's character. The moments of self-reflection, the internal struggles, and the triumphs are all conveyed with a sincerity that transcends the comedic framework of the film. Reeves's ability to navigate the emotional beats of Falco's journey adds a layer of authenticity to the character, allowing audiences to invest in both the humor and the heart of the narrative.

Cultural Impact and Legacy: Keanu Reeves as Shane Falco

Cultural Endurance: Keanu Reeves's portrayal of Shane Falco has endured in the cultural consciousness long after the film's release. The character has become synonymous with the unconventional hero, the underdog who rises to the occasion with a combination of wit, determination, and a touch of self-deprecating humor. Reeves's cultural impact extends beyond the confines of "The Replacements," contributing to the actor's status as a beloved and versatile figure in popular cinema.

Legacy of Leadership: As a cinematic leader, Shane Falco stands as a testament to the enduring appeal of characters who lead not through sheer strength or bravado but through authenticity and determination. Reeves's portrayal adds a layer of humanity to the archetype of the team captain, showcasing that leadership is a journey of self-discovery and growth. The legacy of Shane Falco as a leader endures as a cinematic touchstone for those who appreciate characters that defy traditional expectations.

Conclusion: Keanu Reeves's Touchdown Performance

In conclusion, Keanu Reeves's performance as Shane Falco in "The Replacements" is a touchdown—an exemplary display of charisma, vulnerability, and leadership. Reeves navigates the complexities of Falco's character with a deft touch, infusing the film with a unique blend of humor and emotional resonance. As the charismatic linchpin of a ragtag team, Reeves's Falco transcends the boundaries of sports movie heroes, leaving an indelible mark on the cultural landscape of sports cinema. "The Replacements" stands as a testament to the enduring power of Keanu Reeves's performance, a touchdown that continues to resonate with audiences and reaffirm the actor's status as a cinematic icon.

## Suspension of Disbelief Required

In the realm of sports cinema, certain films demand that audiences set aside their expectations of reality and embrace a narrative that exists in a heightened, often fantastical, space. "The Replacements" (2000), directed by Howard Deutch, is one such cinematic venture that requires viewers to suspend their disbelief and enter a world where a ragtag team of replacement players takes the field during the 1987 NFL Players' Strike. This chapter explores the art of suspension of disbelief within the context of "The Replacements," examining how the film navigates the fine line between the real and the surreal, and how this creative choice enhances the comedic and thematic elements of the narrative.

Introduction: The Cinematic Playground

Defying Reality in Sports Cinema: Sports cinema, by its nature, often mirrors the real-world drama of athletic competition. However, some films choose to defy the constraints of reality, transforming the sports field into a cinematic playground where the improbable and the absurd become narrative assets. "The Replacements" boldly embraces this approach, inviting audiences to enter a world where the rules of conventional sports movies are rewritten in the name of humor, underdog triumph, and the celebration of the human spirit.

Setting the Stage: The 1987 NFL Players' Strike

Historical Context as Creative Canvas: The 1987 NFL Players' Strike serves as the historical backdrop that allows "The Replacements" to take creative liberties. The strike, a real event with significant implications for professional football, becomes the canvas upon which the film paints its narrative. By leveraging this historical context, the filmmakers establish a foundation that both grounds the story in reality and provides the freedom to explore the fantastical elements of the replacement players' journey.

Real-Life Drama as Catalyst: The decision to use a real-life event as a catalyst for fictional storytelling is not uncommon in sports cinema. However, "The Replacements" takes this a step further by not merely depicting the strike but using it as a springboard for a narrative that defies the norms of traditional sports dramas. The suspension of disbelief begins with the premise that replacement players, with little to no professional experience, could seamlessly step into the shoes of seasoned NFL athletes.

The Ragtag Team: From Sumo Wrestler to Welsh Soccer Player

Eccentricity as Narrative Device: The roster of replacement players in "The Replacements" is a mosaic of eccentricity—an ensemble that includes a former sumo wrestler, a Welsh soccer player, a convict with a penchant for violence, and a deaf player, among others. The decision to populate the team with characters that defy traditional sports movie archetypes serves as a key element in the suspension of disbelief. Each player's unique background and skill set contribute to the film's comedic tapestry, simultaneously challenging and embracing the audience's willingness to accept the improbable.

Unconventional Talents on Display: The film strategically introduces the replacement players' unconventional talents, turning them into comedic assets and tools for on-field success. Whether it's the sumo wrestler's agility, the Welsh soccer player's precision, or the convict's raw aggression, each player's skills become exaggerated elements that amplify the film's departure from reality. The narrative invites viewers to revel in the absurdity of a team forged from such disparate backgrounds and talents.

Keanu Reeves as Shane Falco: The Ultimate Underdog Leader

Falco's Backstory: The heart of "The Replacements" lies in the character of Shane Falco, played by Keanu Reeves. Falco's backstory as a former college football star who crumbled under pressure sets the stage for his unlikely journey to redemption. Reeves's portrayal of Falco adds a layer of emotional depth to the film, enhancing the suspension of disbelief by presenting a hero with flaws and vulnerabilities, traits that might seem incongruent with the typical sports movie protagonist.

The Reluctant Hero: Reeves's Falco is the reluctant hero who must overcome his past failures and doubts to lead the ragtag team to success. The narrative choice to position Falco as a reluctant leader adds to the suspension of disbelief, as audiences witness a character who, on the surface, lacks the conventional qualities of a charismatic sports movie captain. Reeves's ability to convey Falco's internal struggles contributes to the authenticity of the character, making his transformation all the more compelling.

On-Field Antics: Comedic Plays and Unorthodox Strategies

Inventive Playbook: "The Replacements" introduces an inventive playbook that defies the conventions of real football strategy. From the "Ole!" play to the "Annexation of Puerto Rico," the film's on-field antics serve as a focal point for the suspension of disbelief. Reeves's portrayal of Falco as the quarterback orchestrating these unorthodox plays adds a layer of humor and incredulity. The film challenges viewers to set aside their expectations of realistic football gameplay and embrace the comedic exaggeration of on-field strategies.

Physical Comedy and Theatrical Flourishes: Reeves's physical commitment to the role amplifies the film's reliance on physical comedy and theatrical flourishes during on-field sequences. From slapstick moments to exaggerated reactions, the performances of Reeves and the ensemble cast contribute to the film's larger-than-life comedic atmosphere. This departure from the physical realism of actual football games reinforces the film's commitment to a heightened, theatrical version of the sport.

Romantic Subplot: Balancing Heart with Hilarity

Romance Amidst Chaos: The romantic subplot between Falco and Annabelle Farrell, played by Brooke Langton, introduces an additional layer of narrative complexity. While grounded in emotional sincerity, this subplot contributes to the film's overall suspension of disbelief. The idea that a romantic connection could bloom amidst the chaos of a high-stakes football season featuring replacement players adds to the film's whimsical tone. Reeves's chemistry with Langton helps sell this romantic dynamic, creating a balance between heartwarming moments and the film's overall comedic ethos.

Realism vs. Escapism: Navigating the Fine Line

Embracing Escapism: "The Replacements" unapologetically embraces escapism, inviting audiences to revel in a world where the rules of reality are bent for the sake of entertainment. The film positions itself as a cinematic escape, offering a respite from the constraints of real-life football dynamics and inviting viewers to engage with a narrative that exists in a realm of heightened imagination. The suspension of disbelief becomes not just a narrative device but a contract between filmmakers and audiences, a shared agreement to enter a world where the improbable is not just possible but celebrated.

Balancing with Emotional Resonance: Despite its commitment to escapism, "The Replacements" recognizes the importance of emotional resonance. Reeves's portrayal of Falco ensures that, amidst the comedic chaos, there are moments of genuine emotion and character growth. The film navigates the fine line between farce and heart, using the suspension of disbelief as a tool to amplify both the humor and the humanity of the narrative. The result is a sports comedy that, while fantastical in its premise, remains grounded in the emotional arcs of its characters.

Cultural Impact: The Legacy of Suspension of Disbelief

Enduring Appeal: "The Replacements" has left an enduring impact on audiences, its legacy defined by the enduring appeal of its comedic and fantastical elements. The film's willingness to ask viewers to suspend their disbelief has contributed to its status as a cult classic within the sports comedy genre. The eclectic mix of humor, unconventional characters, and a charismatic lead performance by Keanu Reeves has solidified the film's place in the pantheon of sports cinema that defies conventional expectations.

Contribution to Sports Comedy: Within the broader landscape of sports comedies, "The Replacements" stands as a testament to the power of suspension of disbelief in enhancing the comedic experience. The film's legacy is not merely defined by its deviation from realistic sports portrayals but by its boldness in embracing the fantastical. This contribution has influenced subsequent sports comedies, inspiring filmmakers to explore the boundaries of reality and imagination within the genre.

Conclusion: Theatrical Fantasy on the Gridiron

In conclusion, "The Replacements" is a theatrical fantasy on the gridiron, a film that demands the audience's willing suspension of disbelief for the sake of comedic joy and underdog triumph. Keanu Reeves's portrayal of Shane Falco, the ragtag team's reluctant leader, anchors the film in a blend of humor and emotional resonance. The suspension of disbelief becomes a contract between filmmakers and viewers, a shared journey into a world where the improbable not only happens but is celebrated with gusto. As the film continues to entertain new generations of audiences, its legacy is not just in its comedic prowess but in its boldness to redefine the boundaries of sports cinema, inviting viewers to embrace the fantastical on the hallowed grounds of the football field.

## Chapter 6: Any Given Sunday (1999)
## Oliver Stone's Hyperkinetic Football Epic

In the annals of sports cinema, certain films transcend the conventional boundaries of storytelling, propelling audiences into a hyperkinetic and visually stunning world that mirrors the intensity of athletic competition. "Any Given Sunday" (1999), directed by the enigmatic Oliver Stone, stands as a prime example of such a cinematic venture. This chapter explores the hyperkinetic nature of Stone's football epic, delving into the director's distinctive style, the frenetic energy infused into the narrative, and the visual techniques that elevate the film beyond the realm of traditional sports dramas.

Introduction: The Fusion of Football and Stone's Aesthetic

Oliver Stone's Cinematic Signature: From "Platoon" to "JFK" and "Natural Born Killers," Oliver Stone is renowned for his visually arresting and thematically dense approach to filmmaking. "Any Given Sunday" marks Stone's foray into the world of sports cinema, and his distinctive style becomes a powerful force that transforms the football field into a canvas of hyperkinetic energy. This chapter examines how Stone's cinematic signature is interwoven with the narrative fabric of "Any Given Sunday," creating a visceral and intense experience for viewers.

Setting the Stage: A League on the Brink

Chaos and Conflict: The narrative backdrop of "Any Given Sunday" is a fictional professional football league on the brink of chaos and upheaval. Stone strategically positions the league's internal struggles as a reflection of the external pressures facing modern sports. This setting becomes the crucible through which the hyperkinetic energy of the film is unleashed. Stone's choice to depict football not just as a game but as a microcosm of societal conflicts lays the foundation for the film's thematic depth and visual dynamism.

The Interconnected Tapestry: Stone weaves an interconnected tapestry of characters, conflicts, and larger-than-life scenarios that mirror the chaos and spectacle of professional football. The film's hyperkinetic nature is not confined to the playing field; it permeates every aspect of the narrative, from locker room dynamics to the high-stakes business dealings that shape the fate of the league. Stone's ability to create a cinematic world where every frame pulsates with energy contributes to the film's immersive quality.

Visual Style: A Symphony of Motion and Chaos

Dynamic Cinematography: Stone's hyperkinetic approach is evident in the film's dynamic cinematography, which captures the speed, power, and visceral impact of football. The camera becomes a participant in the action, moving with the agility of a seasoned athlete to convey the intensity of each play. Stone employs a mix of handheld cameras, sweeping tracking shots, and rapid edits to immerse viewers in the kinetic energy of the game. The result is a visual symphony that mirrors the ebb and flow of a football match.

Montages and Intercutting: Montages and intercutting are prominent features of Stone's visual style in "Any Given Sunday." These techniques create a sense of simultaneity, showcasing multiple storylines and perspectives in rapid succession. Whether it's the chaos of a game, the emotional highs and lows of the characters, or the strategic machinations behind the scenes, Stone uses montage to layer the narrative with complexity and urgency. The film's hyperkinetic editing elevates it beyond the traditional sports drama, creating a sensory experience that mirrors the unpredictability of the sport itself.

The Soundscape: Rhythms of Impact and Intensity

Score and Sound Design: The sonic landscape of "Any Given Sunday" complements its visual dynamism. Stone collaborates with composers Richard Horowitz and Paul Kelly to craft a score that mirrors the rhythms of impact and intensity on the football field. The pounding beats, frenetic tempo, and electronic elements contribute to the film's hyperkinetic atmosphere. Sound design becomes a crucial element in conveying the visceral experience of the sport, with bone-crushing tackles, roaring crowds, and the pulse of adrenaline permeating every scene.

Voiceovers and Commentary: Stone employs voiceovers and sports commentary as narrative devices that enhance the film's hyperkinetic nature. These elements provide insight into the minds of the characters, offering a commentary on the high-stakes world of professional football. The overlapping voices, rapid-fire commentary, and internal monologues contribute to the film's sense of urgency and chaos. Stone's use of sound becomes a narrative tool that propels the story forward and immerses viewers in the relentless pace of the football season.

### Character Dynamics: Intensity in Performance

All-Star Ensemble: "Any Given Sunday" boasts an all-star ensemble cast led by Al Pacino, Cameron Diaz, Jamie Foxx, and Dennis Quaid. Stone directs these performers with a focus on intensity and raw emotion, eliciting powerhouse performances that mirror the hyperkinetic energy of the narrative. The characters become conduits for the film's themes of ambition, power struggles, and the toll of professional sports. Stone's direction encourages the actors to tap into the emotional and physical demands of their roles, contributing to the overall intensity of the film.

Pacino's Commanding Presence: Al Pacino's portrayal of Coach Tony D'Amato is a central element in the film's hyperkinetic tapestry. Pacino's commanding presence, impassioned speeches, and physicality as a coach mirror the tumultuous nature of the football world. Stone and Pacino collaborate to create a character whose journey becomes emblematic of the film's themes, and the actor's ability to convey both vulnerability and authority adds depth to the hyperkinetic narrative.

### Themes of Ambition and Sacrifice: Collateral Damage in Pursuit of Victory

Ambition and Its Consequences: Stone uses the hyperkinetic energy of "Any Given Sunday" to explore themes of ambition and the collateral damage incurred in the pursuit of victory. The film's narrative follows characters driven by ambition, be it for personal success, financial gain, or the quest for glory on the field. Stone portrays the consequences of unchecked ambition, showcasing the toll it takes on relationships, health, and the very fabric of the sport.

Physical Toll on Athletes: The hyperkinetic nature of the football sequences is not merely a stylistic choice but a thematic one. Stone emphasizes the physical toll of the sport on the athletes, underscoring the sacrifices made in the name of competition. Bone-jarring tackles, injuries, and the grueling nature of the game become visual metaphors for the sacrifices required to succeed in professional football. Stone's approach challenges viewers to confront the harsh realities of the sport, even as they are swept up in its kinetic energy.

Theatrical Flourishes: Stone's Theatrical Touch on Familiar Tropes

Subverting Sports Movie Tropes: "Any Given Sunday" takes familiar sports movie tropes and subverts them through Stone's theatrical flourishes. The film embraces the melodrama of the genre while infusing it with a heightened sense of reality. Stone's approach is not to replicate the conventional underdog narrative but to deconstruct and reconstruct it within the hyperkinetic framework of the film. The result is a sports drama that feels both familiar and refreshingly innovative.

Monologues and Theatricality: Stone incorporates monologues and theatrical elements that elevate the film beyond the boundaries of realism. Pacino's iconic "Inches" speech encapsulates this theatricality, serving as a rallying cry that transcends the immediate context of the game. Stone uses these moments to inject philosophical and existential themes into the narrative, inviting viewers to contemplate the broader significance of football as a metaphor for life's battles. The film's theatrical flourishes become moments of reflection and introspection within the frenetic pace of the narrative.

### Conclusion: Any Given Sunday's Cinematic Legacy

In conclusion, "Any Given Sunday" stands as a cinematic tour de force that fuses the hyperkinetic vision of Oliver Stone with the dynamic and visceral world of professional football. The film's impact goes beyond its portrayal of the sport; it becomes a reflection of the chaotic, intense, and often brutal nature of life itself. Stone's distinctive style, coupled with a powerhouse ensemble cast, creates a sports drama that defies conventions and invites viewers into a visually stunning and emotionally charged experience. "Any Given Sunday" is more than a football movie; it's a hyperkinetic exploration of ambition, sacrifice, and the relentless pursuit of victory that continues to resonate with audiences as a cinematic classic within the sports genre.

### Al Pacino Commands as a Beleaguered Coach

In the realm of sports cinema, certain performances transcend the screen, becoming indelible portrayals that capture the essence of a character and elevate the narrative to new heights. Al Pacino's portrayal of Coach Tony D'Amato in "Any Given Sunday" (1999) is one such performance. This chapter delves into Pacino's commanding presence, exploring how he brings depth, complexity, and a sense of beleaguered authority to the character, making Coach D'Amato not just a coach on the sidelines but a symbol of resilience, redemption, and the tumultuous world of professional football.

Introduction: The Coach as Central Figure

The Role of the Coach: In sports films, the coach often serves as a central figure, guiding the narrative and the team toward triumph or redemption. In "Any Given Sunday," Al Pacino takes on the role of Coach Tony D'Amato, a seasoned veteran grappling with the changing landscape of professional football. This chapter examines how Pacino's performance transforms Coach D'Amato into a character whose journey mirrors the broader themes of the film and resonates with audiences as a symbol of leadership in the face of adversity.

Establishing Coach D'Amato: A Seasoned Veteran in Crisis

Coach D'Amato's Backstory: From the film's outset, Coach D'Amato is established as a seasoned veteran in the world of professional football. Pacino infuses the character with a sense of history and experience, portraying D'Amato as a man who has weathered the storms of the sport. The coach's backstory becomes a crucial element in understanding his approach to coaching, leadership, and the challenges he faces as the narrative unfolds.

The Changing Landscape: As the film progresses, Coach D'Amato finds himself navigating the changing landscape of the sport. The introduction of new ownership, represented by Christina Pagniacci (Cameron Diaz), brings with it a shift in the team's priorities—from traditional values to a more business-oriented approach. Pacino's performance captures the coach's struggle to adapt to this evolution while holding onto the principles that define his coaching philosophy.

Pacino's Commanding Presence: Authority and Vulnerability

Physicality and Vocal Intensity: Pacino's commanding presence is evident from the moment he steps onto the screen as Coach D'Amato. The actor infuses the character with a physicality that mirrors the intensity of the sport. Whether pacing the sidelines, delivering impassioned speeches, or engaging in confrontations, Pacino's body language becomes an extension of the coach's beleaguered authority. The actor's vocal intensity adds another layer, conveying both the gravitas and vulnerability of a coach facing the twilight of his career.

Balancing Authority and Humanity: One of the strengths of Pacino's portrayal is the delicate balance between authority and humanity. Coach D'Amato is not a one-dimensional figure but a man grappling with the pressures of coaching, personal losses, and the evolving dynamics of the sport. Pacino navigates this complexity with nuance, allowing the audience to see the coach not just as a symbol of authority but as a human being with flaws, regrets, and a deep passion for the game.

Emotional Arc: Resilience and Redemption

Crises and Setbacks: Coach D'Amato's journey in "Any Given Sunday" is marked by a series of crises and setbacks, both personal and professional. From the team's struggles on the field to conflicts with the new ownership, D'Amato faces challenges that test his resilience and commitment to his coaching principles. Pacino's portrayal ensures that each setback is felt not just as a plot point but as a personal blow to the coach, adding emotional weight to the character's arc.

Redemption and Reinvention: As the narrative unfolds, Coach D'Amato experiences moments of redemption and reinvention. Pacino infuses these moments with a mix of triumph and vulnerability, showcasing the coach's ability to adapt and overcome. Whether it's nurturing the talent of a new quarterback, Willie Beamen (Jamie Foxx), or defying the expectations of the league, D'Amato's journey becomes one of rediscovery and reaffirmation. Pacino's performance elevates these moments, making them pivotal in the coach's quest for redemption.

Iconic Speeches: Pacino's Theatrical Flourishes

Inches Speech: One of the defining moments of Pacino's performance as Coach D'Amato is the iconic "Inches" speech. Delivered with theatrical flair and emotional intensity, the speech becomes a rallying cry for the team and a symbolic declaration of the coach's philosophy. Pacino's delivery infuses the words with a visceral power, transcending the immediate context of the game and becoming a moment of profound reflection on life's battles. The Inches speech stands as a testament to Pacino's ability to use theatrical flourishes to amplify the emotional impact of the narrative.

Philosophical Monologues: Throughout the film, Pacino engages in philosophical monologues that add depth to Coach D'Amato's character. Whether reflecting on the nature of the sport, the sacrifices of the players, or the existential challenges faced by individuals in pursuit of greatness, these monologues showcase Pacino's talent for infusing dialogue with meaning and resonance. The coach's reflections become moments of introspection within the hyperkinetic pace of the film, and Pacino's delivery ensures that they resonate with authenticity.

Dynamics with the Ensemble Cast: Chemistry and Conflict

Chemistry with Jamie Foxx: Pacino's chemistry with Jamie Foxx, who plays quarterback Willie Beamen, is a standout aspect of "Any Given Sunday." The mentor-mentee dynamic between Coach D'Amato and Beamen adds layers to both characters, and Pacino's performance ensures that the evolving relationship feels authentic. The clash of generations, coaching styles, and personal philosophies becomes a focal point for both characters, and Pacino's scenes with Foxx showcase the actor's ability to navigate dynamic and often conflict-laden relationships.

Conflict with Christina Pagniacci: The conflict between Coach D'Amato and team owner Christina Pagniacci, played by Cameron Diaz, is another dimension of the coach's journey.

Pacino and Diaz engage in scenes of verbal sparring and power dynamics, and Pacino's performance ensures that the coach's resistance to the changing culture of the team feels grounded in principles rather than mere obstinacy. The dynamics with Diaz's character add a layer of tension to the narrative, and Pacino's commanding presence holds its own in the face of corporate pressure.

Impact and Legacy: Coach D'Amato Beyond the Screen

Symbol of Resilience: Coach D'Amato, as portrayed by Al Pacino, has become a symbol of resilience and determination in the realm of sports cinema. The character's journey, marked by triumphs, failures, and moments of profound introspection, resonates with audiences as a reflection of the challenges faced by coaches in the real world. Pacino's performance ensures that Coach D'Amato transcends the confines of fiction, becoming an enduring symbol of leadership and perseverance.

Legacy in Sports Films: Pacino's portrayal of Coach D'Amato has left an indelible mark on the landscape of sports films. The character's memorable speeches, emotional arc, and the nuanced performance by Pacino have contributed to the enduring legacy of "Any Given Sunday" within the genre. The film's impact extends beyond its initial release, as Coach D'Amato continues to be cited in discussions of iconic coaching portrayals in cinema.

Conclusion: Pacino's Coach D'Amato as Cinematic Archetype

In conclusion, Al Pacino's portrayal of Coach Tony D'Amato in "Any Given Sunday" stands as a cinematic archetype of coaching in the face of adversity. Pacino's commanding presence, nuanced performance, and the emotional depth he brings to the character elevate Coach D'Amato beyond the conventions of sports cinema. The beleaguered coach becomes a symbol of resilience, redemption, and the enduring spirit of those who navigate the tumultuous world of professional football. Pacino's contribution to the film cements Coach D'Amato as an iconic figure, ensuring that his impact resonates not just within the narrative of "Any Given Sunday" but in the broader tapestry of sports films.

### Exposing the Brutality Behind the Glamor

In the realm of sports cinema, the portrayal of professional football has often been glamorized, capturing the thrilling moments of victory and the glory of the game. However, Oliver Stone's "Any Given Sunday" (1999) takes a bold departure from this conventional narrative, opting to expose the inherent brutality that lurks behind the glamorized façade of football. This chapter delves into how the film, under Stone's direction, strips away the veneer of glamour to reveal the visceral, often harsh, realities of the sport. From bone-crushing hits on the field to the cutthroat business dealings off it, "Any Given Sunday" becomes a cinematic exploration of the brutality that underpins the world of professional football.

Introduction: Unmasking the Glittering Facade

Glamor in Sports Cinema: Sports films, particularly those centered around football, have a tradition of celebrating the heroics, triumphs, and camaraderie of the game. The gladiatorial spectacle of the gridiron, framed by slow-motion shots and soaring musical scores, has often taken center stage. "Any Given Sunday," however, sets out on a different course. Under Stone's directorial vision, the film unapologetically exposes the brutality beneath the glamorous surface, challenging viewers to confront the physical, emotional, and ethical toll of professional football.

The Physical Brutality: Football as a Contact Sport

The Power of Cinematic Realism: Oliver Stone, known for his commitment to cinematic realism, approaches the depiction of football in "Any Given Sunday" with an unflinching lens. The physical brutality of the sport is presented in its raw, unfiltered form. From bone-jarring tackles to the grueling toll on players' bodies, Stone's approach aims to immerse the audience in the harsh realities of football. Cinematography, sound design, and editing work in tandem to convey the impact of each collision, disrupting the romanticized image of football as mere spectacle.

Injury Montages: One of the techniques used by Stone to expose the physical brutality is the inclusion of injury montages. These sequences are a stark departure from the conventional highlight reels seen in sports films. Instead of celebrating moments of athletic prowess, the film lingers on the aftermath of the game—the battered bodies, the injuries, and the toll exacted on players. Stone's use of montages becomes a narrative device to underscore the high stakes and physical sacrifices inherent in the pursuit of victory.

Emotional Brutality: Struggles Beyond the Field

Fractured Relationships: While "Any Given Sunday" captures the physical brutality on the field, it equally explores the emotional toll that the sport extracts from its participants. Stone portrays fractured relationships, strained bonds between players and coaches, and the toll that the relentless pursuit of success takes on personal lives. The emotional brutality becomes a thematic undercurrent, weaving through the narrative to expose the vulnerabilities and fractured psyches of those immersed in the world of professional football.

Players as Commodities: The film sheds light on the emotional brutality inherent in the commodification of players.

Stone presents a world where athletes are not just athletes; they are commodities bought and sold in the marketplace of professional sports. This dehumanizing aspect of the industry is exposed through the struggles of characters like Willie Beamen (Jamie Foxx), whose journey reflects the emotional toll of being treated as a product rather than a person. Stone challenges the audience to confront the dehumanization that often accompanies the pursuit of glory in professional football.

Ethical Brutality: The Dark Side of Competition

Performance-Enhancing Drugs: "Any Given Sunday" delves into the ethical brutality that underlies the hyper-competitive nature of professional football. The use of performance-enhancing drugs becomes a focal point, challenging the pristine image of athletes. Stone's depiction is not one of moralizing but of presenting a nuanced exploration of the choices players make in a high-stakes environment. The film confronts the ethical complexities surrounding the quest for peak performance, acknowledging the pressures and temptations that can lead athletes down morally ambiguous paths.

Business vs. Integrity: Stone exposes the ethical brutality not only within the realm of competition but also in the corporate boardrooms that dictate the trajectory of football franchises. The clash between the business-driven mindset, embodied by team owner Christina Pagniacci (Cameron Diaz), and the traditional values of Coach Tony D'Amato (Al Pacino) becomes a microcosm of the ethical struggles within the sport. The film questions whether the pursuit of victory should come at the expense of integrity, raising ethical dilemmas that resonate far beyond the confines of the football field.

### Behind-the-Scenes Brutality: Cutthroat Business of Football

Ownership Power Dynamics: "Any Given Sunday" explores the cutthroat nature of the business side of professional football, unmasking the power dynamics that shape the destiny of teams. Stone portrays the struggles between team owners, the tug-of-war for control, and the impact of business decisions on the players and coaching staff. By pulling back the curtain on the ownership dynamics, the film exposes a level of brutality where success is measured not just in touchdowns but in financial gains and franchise value.

Coaching Carousel: The film sheds light on the coaching carousel, where the pressure for immediate success can lead to ruthless decisions regarding coaching staff. Coaches, portrayed as expendable commodities, face the constant threat of being replaced in the pursuit of better results. Stone's narrative explores the human cost of such decisions, emphasizing the emotional and professional toll on those caught in the whirlwind of the coaching carousel.

### Conclusion: A Cinematic Revelation of Football Realities

In conclusion, "Any Given Sunday" stands as a cinematic revelation, unmasking the brutal realities that lie beneath the glamorous exterior of professional football. Oliver Stone's bold approach challenges the conventions of sports cinema, presenting a narrative that confronts the physical, emotional, and ethical brutality that pervades the world of football. By exposing the toll on players' bodies, the emotional struggles beyond the field, and the cutthroat nature of the business, the film becomes a provocative exploration of the sport's multifaceted brutality. "Any Given Sunday" serves as a stark reminder that, behind the dazzling spectacle of the gridiron, there exists a world defined by sacrifice, resilience, and the unrelenting pursuit of victory at any cost.

## Stone's Theatrical Flourishes Energize Familiar Tropes

In the realm of sports cinema, where the narrative beats of triumph and adversity often follow a familiar playbook, Oliver Stone's "Any Given Sunday" (1999) emerges as a distinctive entry that defies conventions. This chapter explores how Stone's directorial vision infuses theatrical flourishes into the film, breathing new life into familiar sports tropes. From visually dynamic football sequences to the heightened emotional drama off the field, Stone employs his signature style to energize the narrative, offering audiences a cinematic experience that transcends the boundaries of traditional sports storytelling.

Introduction: Redefining the Sports Genre

Evolution of Sports Cinema: Sports cinema has evolved over the years, offering audiences narratives that celebrate the human spirit, resilience, and the pursuit of excellence. While many sports films adhere to established tropes and storytelling conventions, "Any Given Sunday" marks a departure from the norm. Oliver Stone, known for his bold and unconventional approach to filmmaking, injects the sports genre with his unique brand of theatricality, redefining how the stories of athletes, coaches, and the sport itself are portrayed on screen.

Visual Dynamism: Football as Hyperkinetic Spectacle

The Kinetic Energy of Football: One of the ways in which Stone's theatrical flourishes manifest is in the visual dynamism of the football sequences. The director employs a hyperkinetic style, using rapid editing, dynamic camera movements, and visceral sound design to capture the intense energy of the game. Each play becomes a spectacle, not just in the outcome but in the kinetic experience of the sport itself. Stone's approach transcends traditional sports cinematography, transforming football into a hyperreal, almost surreal, visual feast.

On-Field Chaos and Choreography: Stone's directorial choices bring chaos and choreography to the on-field action. The football sequences are not just about capturing the plays but about immersing the audience in the physicality, speed, and strategic intricacies of the sport. The chaos of the game is choreographed with precision, creating a sensory experience that goes beyond the conventional depiction of football on screen. Through rapid cuts, close-ups, and innovative camera angles, Stone transforms the gridiron into a stage for a visually dynamic and emotionally charged performance.

Emotional Intensity: Theatricality Off the Field

Character Drama and Theatrical Flourishes: While the football sequences showcase Stone's kinetic approach, the theatrical flourishes extend into the emotional drama off the field. Stone heightens the emotional intensity of character interactions, using stylized visuals, intense close-ups, and dramatic lighting to amplify the emotional stakes. The director's theatrical touch transforms dialogue exchanges into heightened moments of conflict, passion, and revelation, transcending the naturalism often associated with sports dramas.

Confrontations and Verbal Sparring: One notable aspect of Stone's theatrical approach is the emphasis on confrontations and verbal sparring between characters. Whether it's Coach Tony D'Amato (Al Pacino) clashing with team owner Christina Pagniacci (Cameron Diaz) or the emotional exchanges between players, Stone infuses these moments with theatrical flair. The characters' conflicts become performances in their own right, with dialogue delivered as impassioned monologues that echo the intensity of the on-field clashes.

Theatrical Flourishes in Character Portrayals

Al Pacino's Theatrical Presence: Stone's theatrical flourishes find a perfect canvas in the larger-than-life performances of the cast. Al Pacino, in particular, brings a theatrical presence to his portrayal of Coach Tony D'Amato. The actor's delivery, marked by dramatic pauses, emphatic gestures, and a powerful vocal presence, elevates D'Amato from a traditional coach archetype to a theatrical figure commanding attention. Pacino's performance becomes a focal point for Stone's theatrical vision, creating a character whose presence mirrors the heightened drama of the narrative.

Jamie Foxx's Dynamic Range: Jamie Foxx, playing quarterback Willie Beamen, contributes to the film's theatricality with his dynamic range. From the exuberance of success to the depths of personal struggles, Foxx infuses Beamen with a theatrical flair that mirrors the emotional rollercoaster of professional football. The character's journey becomes a theatrical performance, and Foxx's ability to navigate the highs and lows with dramatic intensity adds layers to the film's exploration of the human experience within the sporting arena.

Symbolic Imagery: Metaphors and Allegory

Symbolism on the Field: Stone's theatrical touch extends to the symbolic imagery woven into the narrative. The football field becomes a symbolic stage where the struggles, triumphs, and conflicts of the characters play out. Through visual metaphors, such as the inches speech delivered by Coach D'Amato, Stone elevates the on-field action beyond a literal representation of the sport. The field becomes a canvas for allegory, where the inches represent more than just yardage—they embody the larger battles of life, ambition, and resilience.

Visual Allegory Beyond the Field: Beyond the football field, Stone employs visual allegory to enhance the narrative. The use of recurring motifs, such as water symbolism representing rebirth and renewal, adds layers of meaning to the film. These visual allegories serve as a theatrical device, inviting audiences to engage with the narrative on a symbolic level. Stone's incorporation of visual metaphors elevates "Any Given Sunday" from a sports drama to a cinematic exploration of universal themes.

Musical Score: Heightening Emotional Beats

Robbie Robertson's Score: The theatricality of "Any Given Sunday" is further accentuated by the musical score composed by Robbie Robertson. The score becomes a crucial element in enhancing emotional beats, underscoring the intensity of on-field clashes and off-field drama. Robertson's use of anthemic compositions and rhythmic motifs contributes to the film's overall sense of theatrical grandeur, turning the score into a sonic backdrop that amplifies the emotional resonance of key moments.

Integration of Contemporary Music: In addition to the original score, Stone incorporates contemporary music into the film, further contributing to its theatrical atmosphere. The use of songs by artists like LL Cool J and Puff Daddy adds a modern, dynamic layer to the soundtrack. Stone's choice to integrate popular music reflects the film's departure from traditional sports drama conventions, embracing a more contemporary and theatrical sensibility.

Conclusion: A Theatrical Triumph in Sports Cinema

In conclusion, "Any Given Sunday" stands as a theatrical triumph within the realm of sports cinema. Oliver Stone's directorial vision infuses the film with kinetic energy, emotional intensity, and symbolic depth that transcend the familiar tropes of the genre. From the visual dynamism of football sequences to the heightened emotional drama off the field, Stone's theatrical flourishes redefine how sports stories are told on the big screen. "Any Given Sunday" becomes not just a sports drama but a cinematic experience that challenges, engages, and ultimately transcends the boundaries of traditional sports storytelling. Stone's bold approach cements the film as a testament to the transformative power of theatricality in reimagining the narratives of athletes, coaches, and the sports they inhabit.

## Chapter 7: The Blind Side (2009)
## Bringing Michael Oher's Life to the Screen

In the landscape of sports films, "The Blind Side" (2009) emerges as a unique entry that transcends the traditional boundaries of the genre. This chapter delves into the intricate process of bringing Michael Oher's life to the screen, exploring the challenges, creative decisions, and the profound impact of Sandra Bullock's Oscar-winning performance. From the adaptation of Michael Lewis's book to the portrayal of real-life events, "The Blind Side" navigates the complexities of storytelling, race, and socio-economic dynamics to present a compelling narrative that extends beyond the football field.

Introduction: The Unlikely Tale of Michael Oher

From Reality to Reel: "The Blind Side" unfolds as a cinematic journey that takes inspiration from the real-life story of Michael Oher. The film's narrative is grounded in Oher's experiences, from his challenging childhood to his unexpected journey to becoming an NFL player. This introduction sets the stage for an exploration of the intricate process of adapting a true story for the screen and the responsibilities that come with portraying real people and events.

Adapting Michael Lewis's Book: Narrative Choices

Michael Lewis's Source Material: "The Blind Side" finds its roots in Michael Lewis's nonfiction book, "The Blind Side: Evolution of a Game," which delves into the evolution of offensive football strategies in the NFL. The book, however, goes beyond the technical aspects of the sport, intertwining the narrative with Michael Oher's life story. The adaptation process involves selecting and shaping the narrative, deciding which aspects of Oher's life to emphasize, and weaving them into a cohesive cinematic experience.

Shifting Focus to Oher's Journey: One of the key narrative choices in adapting the book is the decision to shift the focus from the broader context of football strategy evolution to Michael Oher's personal journey. The film navigates the challenges of balancing the sports elements with Oher's life narrative, ensuring that the audience connects with the human story at the heart of the film. This shift in focus reflects the filmmakers' intent to create a character-driven narrative that goes beyond the technicalities of the sport.

Casting and Characterization: Sandra Bullock as Leigh Anne Tuohy

Sandra Bullock's Transformation: A pivotal aspect of bringing Michael Oher's life to the screen is the casting of Sandra Bullock as Leigh Anne Tuohy. Bullock's portrayal earned her critical acclaim and an Academy Award for Best Actress. This section explores the transformation of Bullock into Tuohy, examining the actor's dedication to the role, the challenges of portraying a real person, and the impact of her performance on the film's reception.

Capturing Leigh Anne Tuohy's Essence: Sandra Bullock's portrayal goes beyond a mere physical transformation. The actor delves into capturing the essence of Leigh Anne Tuohy—her mannerisms, speech patterns, and the nuances that define her character. Bullock's performance becomes a key element in grounding the film, providing a relatable and authentic anchor to the narrative. The chapter delves into how Bullock's dedication to authenticity contributes to the film's overall success.

Navigating Sensitive Themes: Race and Socio-Economic Dynamics

Race in "The Blind Side": The film grapples with the sensitive theme of race, portraying the dynamics of a white family taking in a Black teenager. This section explores how "The Blind Side" handles race, the challenges of depicting real-life racial dynamics, and the impact of these portrayals on the film's reception. From the casting choices to the on-screen interactions, the film navigates a delicate balance in presenting a narrative that delves into racial and socio-economic disparities.

Socio-Economic Dynamics: In addition to race, the film explores socio-economic dynamics, depicting the disparities between the Tuohy family's affluent lifestyle and Michael Oher's impoverished background. The chapter examines how the filmmakers navigate these themes, portraying the complexities of privilege, charity, and the transformative power of compassion. The film's portrayal of socio-economic disparities becomes a lens through which the audience engages with Oher's journey, highlighting the broader societal issues at play.

Michael Oher's Character Arc: The Intersection of Football and Personal Growth

From Homelessness to NFL Success: "The Blind Side" traces Michael Oher's remarkable journey from homelessness to becoming an NFL player. This section explores the nuances of Oher's character arc, examining the challenges he faces, the impact of the Tuohy family on his life, and the intersection of football with personal growth. The film becomes not just a sports drama but a character-driven narrative that explores resilience, identity, and the transformative power of mentorship.

Balancing Football Action and Personal Narrative: A significant aspect of bringing Oher's life to the screen is the balance between football action and the personal narrative. The filmmakers must engage both sports enthusiasts and general audiences, ensuring that the on-field sequences are dynamic and authentic while maintaining a focus on Oher's personal journey. This section delves into how the film strikes this balance, using football as a backdrop for Oher's broader life story.

Impact Beyond the Screen: Cultural and Social Reverberations

Real-Life Impact: "The Blind Side" extends its impact beyond the confines of the screen, influencing cultural and social conversations. This section explores how the film's portrayal of Michael Oher's journey and the Tuohy family's involvement in his life sparks discussions about privilege, charity, and the role of individuals in addressing societal challenges. The real-life impact of the film becomes a testament to the power of storytelling to evoke reflection and dialogue.

Criticisms and Controversies: While "The Blind Side" receives acclaim for its compelling narrative, it is not without criticisms and controversies. This section examines some of the critiques leveled at the film, including concerns about oversimplification, the "white savior" trope, and debates about the accuracy of certain events. The chapter navigates these complexities, acknowledging the film's cultural significance while addressing the discussions it has sparked.

Conclusion: Michael Oher's Story as Cinematic Inspiration

In conclusion, "The Blind Side" stands as a cinematic exploration of Michael Oher's life, navigating the challenges of adaptation, casting, and portrayal of sensitive themes. The film's success lies not only in its compelling narrative but in its ability to transcend traditional sports drama tropes, offering a nuanced and heartfelt portrayal of resilience, compassion, and personal growth. Michael Oher's story becomes a cinematic inspiration, sparking conversations about race, privilege, and the transformative power of empathy. "The Blind Side" leaves an indelible mark as a film that not only brings a true story to the screen but prompts audiences to reflect on their own roles in creating positive change within their communities.

## Sandra Bullock's Oscar-Winning Performance

In the realm of sports films, standout performances can elevate a movie beyond its narrative and make it an enduring cinematic experience. "The Blind Side" (2009) is no exception, and at the heart of its success is Sandra Bullock's compelling portrayal of Leigh Anne Tuohy. This chapter delves into the nuances of Bullock's Oscar-winning performance, examining the actress's transformative approach to the role, the challenges of portraying a real-life figure, and the impact of her portrayal on the film's reception.

Introduction: The Role of Leigh Anne Tuohy

Characterizing Leigh Anne Tuohy: "The Blind Side" introduces audiences to Leigh Anne Tuohy, a strong-willed and compassionate woman whose life becomes intertwined with that of Michael Oher. The chapter sets the stage by exploring the character of Tuohy, her real-life persona, and the challenges and responsibilities that come with portraying a living, breathing individual on the screen.

Sandra Bullock Takes the Stage

The Unexpected Choice: When Sandra Bullock was cast as Leigh Anne Tuohy, it raised eyebrows and piqued curiosity. Known primarily for her work in romantic comedies, Bullock wasn't an obvious choice for a role in a sports drama rooted in real-life events. This section delves into the unexpected casting decision, exploring how Bullock approached the role and defied expectations to deliver a performance that would redefine her career.

Transformative Commitment: Bullock's commitment to the role goes beyond mere physical transformation. The actress immersed herself in understanding Leigh Anne Tuohy, spending time with the real Tuohy, studying her mannerisms, and internalizing the nuances of her character. This section explores the transformative commitment Bullock brought to the role, shedding light on the dedication required to authentically portray a real person on the screen.

Capturing Leigh Anne's Essence

Balancing Strength and Vulnerability: Leigh Anne Tuohy is a character defined by her strength, resilience, and unwavering determination. Bullock navigates the delicate balance of capturing Tuohy's strong-willed nature while infusing vulnerability into her portrayal. This exploration delves into the nuances of Bullock's performance, examining how she conveys the multifaceted aspects of Tuohy's character.

Speech, Mannerisms, and Accent: A key aspect of Bullock's portrayal is her attention to the details of Leigh Anne Tuohy's speech patterns, mannerisms, and distinct Southern accent. The actress's ability to authentically embody these elements contributes to the immersive quality of her performance. This section dissects how Bullock's meticulous approach to these details enhances the credibility of her portrayal.

Chemistry with Co-Stars: The Tuohy Family Dynamics

Family Dynamics: "The Blind Side" not only focuses on Leigh Anne Tuohy as an individual but also explores the dynamics of the Tuohy family. Bullock's performance extends beyond portraying a singular character to capturing the essence of the family matriarch. This section examines how Bullock establishes chemistry with her on-screen family, portraying the complexities of familial relationships with authenticity and depth.

Dynamic with Quinton Aaron (Michael Oher): Central to the film is the relationship between Leigh Anne Tuohy and Michael Oher, portrayed by Quinton Aaron. Bullock's performance is intricately woven into the dynamics of this central relationship, where her character becomes a guiding force in Oher's life. The exploration delves into how Bullock navigates the emotional beats of this relationship, portraying a mentorship that transcends familial and societal expectations.

Navigating Sensitive Themes: Race, Privilege, and Compassion

Addressing Racial Dynamics: "The Blind Side" delves into sensitive themes, including race, privilege, and compassion. As Leigh Anne Tuohy, Bullock becomes a central figure in navigating these themes. This section explores how Bullock's performance contributes to the film's nuanced portrayal of racial dynamics, examining the challenges and responsibilities that come with depicting real-life socio-cultural complexities.

Privilege and Compassion: The film also tackles issues of privilege and compassion, depicting Tuohy's decision to take in Michael Oher as an act of kindness that transcends racial and socio-economic divides. Bullock's portrayal becomes a lens through which these themes are explored, and this part of the chapter dissects how her performance contributes to the film's commentary on compassion, privilege, and social responsibility.

Oscar-Winning Impact: Critical Acclaim and Cultural Reception

Critical Acclaim: Sandra Bullock's portrayal of Leigh Anne Tuohy earned her widespread critical acclaim, culminating in the pinnacle of recognition—an Academy Award for Best Actress. This section explores the critical reception of Bullock's performance, dissecting reviews, accolades, and the industry's acknowledgment of her transformative work in "The Blind Side."

Cultural Reception and Impact: Beyond critical acclaim, Bullock's performance resonated culturally, sparking conversations about the film's themes and the broader issues it addresses. This section delves into the cultural reception of Bullock's portrayal, examining how her performance contributed to the film's impact on discussions around race, privilege, and compassion.

Legacy and Reflections: Sandra Bullock's Career Evolution

Career Evolution: "The Blind Side" marked a turning point in Sandra Bullock's career, propelling her from the romantic comedy genre into more diverse and challenging roles. This part of the chapter traces the trajectory of Bullock's career evolution post-"The Blind Side," exploring how the film influenced her choices and the broader perception of her as an actress.

Reflections on Leigh Anne Tuohy: Sandra Bullock's portrayal of Leigh Anne Tuohy remains a significant chapter in her filmography. This section explores Bullock's reflections on the character, her impact on audiences, and the enduring legacy of "The Blind Side" in shaping perceptions of sports dramas, real-life adaptations, and the transformative power of exceptional performances.

Conclusion: Sandra Bullock's Defining Performance

In conclusion, Sandra Bullock's Oscar-winning performance in "The Blind Side" stands as a defining moment in sports cinema. Her portrayal of Leigh Anne Tuohy goes beyond a mere depiction of a real person; it becomes a masterclass in transformative acting, nuanced character exploration, and navigating complex themes with sensitivity. Bullock's performance elevates "The Blind Side" from a sports drama to a compelling exploration of humanity, compassion, and the enduring impact of exceptional performances in cinematic storytelling.

## Feel-Good True Story Appeals to Wide Audience

"The Blind Side" (2009) transcends the boundaries of traditional sports dramas, weaving a narrative that not only explores the intricacies of football but also delves into the transformative power of compassion. This chapter delves into the film's unique appeal as a feel-good true story, examining how its universal themes, relatable characters, and heartwarming narrative resonate with a wide audience.

Introduction: The Universal Allure of Feel-Good Stories

The Power of Feel-Good Narratives: Feel-good stories hold a unique place in cinema, offering audiences narratives that inspire, uplift, and leave a lasting impact. "The Blind Side" emerges as a testament to the universal allure of such narratives, combining the elements of a true story with the heartwarming journey of its characters. This introduction sets the stage for an exploration of how the film's feel-good qualities contribute to its broad appeal.

Creating an Emotional Connection

Relatable Characters and Human Experience: One of the key elements that contribute to the feel-good nature of "The Blind Side" is its portrayal of relatable characters navigating the challenges of life. This section explores how characters like Leigh Anne Tuohy, Michael Oher, and the Tuohy family resonate with audiences by tapping into universal aspects of the human experience—compassion, resilience, and the transformative power of human connections.

Personal Journeys and Emotional Resonance: The film weaves together personal journeys that unfold with emotional resonance. Whether it's Michael Oher's path from homelessness to the NFL or Leigh Anne Tuohy's decision to extend compassion beyond societal norms, the characters' arcs contribute to the film's emotional depth. This section examines how these personal journeys create an emotional connection with audiences, fostering empathy and investment in the characters' outcomes.

True Events and Inspirational Storytelling

True Story Adaptation: "The Blind Side" is grounded in real-life events, adapting the story of Michael Oher from Michael Lewis's book of the same name. This section explores how the film's connection to true events enhances its feel-good quality, providing audiences with an inspirational narrative that goes beyond fiction. The authenticity derived from Oher's actual experiences adds weight to the storytelling, making the film more than just a scripted drama.

Inspirational Themes: Inspirational storytelling is a hallmark of feel-good films, and "The Blind Side" is no exception. The film tackles themes of compassion, kindness, and the belief in the potential for positive change. This part of the chapter delves into how the film's inspirational themes contribute to its feel-good appeal, examining the impact of storytelling that uplifts and motivates audiences.

Cinematic Craftsmanship and Visual Appeal

Directorial Choices: John Lee Hancock's directorial choices play a crucial role in shaping the feel-good atmosphere of the film. This section explores how Hancock's approach, from pacing to visual aesthetics, contributes to the overall cinematic experience. The director's ability to balance emotional depth with engaging storytelling enhances the feel-good quality, creating a film that is both visually appealing and emotionally satisfying.

Cinematography and Warm Aesthetics: The film's cinematography employs warm and inviting aesthetics that complement its feel-good narrative. This part of the chapter analyzes the visual elements, including the use of color, framing, and cinematographic techniques, to illustrate how the film's visual appeal enhances the emotional resonance of the story. The warm tones and intimate shots contribute to creating a cinematic world that invites audiences into the characters' lives.

Humor and Heart: Striking the Right Balance

Humorous Moments: Feel-good films often incorporate humor as a means of connecting with audiences and lightening the overall tone. This section explores how "The Blind Side" integrates humor into its narrative, examining the role of comedic moments in balancing the more dramatic aspects of the story. From Leigh Anne Tuohy's no-nonsense attitude to the interactions within the Tuohy family, humor becomes a key component in creating an engaging and enjoyable viewing experience.

Heartfelt Moments: The film's feel-good nature is also rooted in its ability to deliver heartfelt moments that resonate emotionally. This part of the chapter dissects the impactful scenes that evoke joy, empathy, and a sense of shared humanity. Whether it's moments of triumph on the football field or instances of compassion within the Tuohy household, these heartfelt moments contribute to the overall feel-good atmosphere of the film.

Wide Audience Appeal and Cultural Impact

Reaching Diverse Audiences: "The Blind Side" achieves a rare feat by appealing to a wide and diverse audience. This section explores the factors that contribute to the film's ability to resonate with viewers across age groups, backgrounds, and interests. The universal themes of family, resilience, and compassion transcend demographic boundaries, making the film accessible to a broad spectrum of audiences.

Cultural Impact: The cultural impact of "The Blind Side" extends beyond its initial release, shaping conversations about sports, family dynamics, and the capacity for positive change. This part of the chapter examines how the film's feel-good appeal contributes to its enduring cultural impact, influencing discussions about representation in cinema, the power of true stories, and the role of empathy in storytelling.

Criticisms and Debates: Navigating Feel-Good Tropes

Criticisms of Oversimplification: While the film is celebrated for its feel-good qualities, it is not without criticisms. This section explores some of the critiques, including concerns about oversimplification of complex issues, the "white savior" trope, and debates about the accuracy of certain events. The chapter navigates these discussions, acknowledging the film's strengths while addressing the complexities inherent in portraying real-life events.

Conclusion: The Enduring Appeal of "The Blind Side"

In conclusion, "The Blind Side" captivates audiences with its feel-good true story that transcends the conventional boundaries of sports dramas. Through relatable characters, inspirational themes, and a cinematic craftsmanship that balances humor with heart, the film creates an enduring appeal that resonates with a wide and diverse audience. "The Blind Side" stands as a cinematic testament to the uplifting power of storytelling, leaving an indelible mark as a film that not only entertains but also inspires and connects with the shared humanity within us all.

## Racial and Economic Issues Simmer Beneath Uplifting Tale

"The Blind Side" (2009) unfolds as more than a heartwarming sports drama; beneath its uplifting tale lies a complex exploration of racial and economic dynamics. This chapter delves into the nuanced depiction of these issues within the film, examining how they add layers of depth to the narrative, contribute to character development, and spark conversations about privilege, compassion, and societal disparities.

Introduction: The Intersection of Race and Economic Struggle

Beyond the Uplifting Tale: While "The Blind Side" is celebrated for its feel-good narrative, this chapter sets the stage by acknowledging that beneath the uplifting tale lies a nuanced exploration of racial and economic issues. The film navigates the intersection of race and economic struggle, presenting a narrative that goes beyond traditional sports dramas by delving into the complexities of privilege, compassion, and societal disparities.

Portrayal of Michael Oher's Background

Introduction to Michael Oher's Background: The film introduces audiences to Michael Oher, a young Black man navigating the challenges of homelessness and poverty. This section explores how the portrayal of Oher's background sets the stage for a deeper examination of racial and economic dynamics. From his early struggles to his eventual encounter with the Tuohy family, Oher's journey becomes a lens through which these issues are explored.

Navigating Stereotypes: "The Blind Side" consciously navigates the potential pitfalls of racial stereotypes, presenting Oher as an individual with his own agency, dreams, and challenges. This exploration delves into how the film sidesteps common tropes associated with Black characters in cinema, striving for an authentic portrayal that challenges preconceptions and stereotypes.

The Tuohy Family's Affluence and White Privilege

Introduction to the Tuohy Family: The contrast between Michael Oher's impoverished background and the affluence of the Tuohy family becomes a central element in the film's exploration of economic disparities. This section examines how the Tuohy family's wealth and privilege contribute to the overarching narrative, creating a dynamic that highlights the societal gaps between races and economic classes.

White Savior Trope: Critiques and Subversion: As the Tuohy family becomes instrumental in Oher's life, the film grapples with the "white savior" trope. This exploration delves into critiques of the trope within the context of "The Blind Side," analyzing how the film both conforms to and subverts elements of this narrative archetype.

Interpersonal Dynamics: Compassion and Complexity

Compassion as a Driving Force: Compassion serves as a driving force within the narrative, leading Leigh Anne Tuohy to extend support to Michael Oher. This section examines the portrayal of compassion within the film, exploring how it becomes a catalyst for positive change while also acknowledging the complexities inherent in the Tuohy-Oher relationship.

Challenges and Cultural Nuances: "The Blind Side" navigates the challenges and cultural nuances inherent in the cross-cultural relationship between the Tuohy family and Michael Oher. From the nuances of language to the differing cultural perspectives, this exploration delves into how the film addresses the complexities of bridging racial and economic divides.

Subtle Racism and Microaggressions

Subtle Racism in Suburban Contexts: While set in a suburban environment, the film subtly portrays the existence of racism within seemingly idyllic communities. This section explores how "The Blind Side" captures subtle instances of racism and microaggressions, illustrating that even in affluent neighborhoods, racial biases persist.

Educational System Dynamics: Michael Oher's journey within the educational system becomes a microcosm of larger racial disparities in education. This part of the chapter examines how the film portrays the challenges faced by Oher within the educational system, shedding light on institutional biases and the impact of systemic inequalities.

Media and Public Perception: Racial Narratives

Media Portrayals and Racial Stereotypes: The film reflects on how media portrayals shape public perception, particularly regarding race. This section explores how the media's depiction of Michael Oher contributes to broader racial narratives, addressing the impact of stereotypes perpetuated by news coverage and public discourse.

Public Reactions and Stereotype Reinforcement: "The Blind Side" delves into the public reactions and perceptions of Michael Oher, reflecting the real-world consequences of racial stereotypes. This exploration analyzes how the film depicts the reinforcement of stereotypes through public discourse and societal expectations.

Complexities of Economic Disparities

Economic Struggles Beyond Oher's Story: While Oher's journey provides a focal point, the film also explores economic struggles beyond his personal narrative. This section delves into how the film portrays the broader economic disparities within the community, touching on issues of housing, education, and employment opportunities.

The Influence of Economic Status on Opportunities: "The Blind Side" emphasizes how economic status can influence opportunities and access to resources. This exploration delves into the systemic challenges faced by individuals from lower economic backgrounds and the film's portrayal of how economic disparities impact life trajectories.

Conclusion: Navigating the Undercurrents

In conclusion, "The Blind Side" skillfully navigates the undercurrents of racial and economic dynamics, adding layers of complexity to its uplifting tale. Through the portrayal of Michael Oher's background, the Tuohy family's affluence, interpersonal dynamics, subtle racism, media narratives, and economic struggles, the film becomes a nuanced exploration of societal disparities. "The Blind Side" invites audiences to reflect on the intersections of race and economic privilege, challenging preconceptions and fostering conversations about compassion, systemic inequalities, and the potential for positive change.

## Chapter 8: Invincible (2006)
## Vince Papale's Improbable NFL Dream Comes True

"Invincible" (2006) tells the inspirational true story of Vince Papale, an ordinary man who defied the odds to achieve his dream of playing in the NFL. This chapter explores the cinematic portrayal of Papale's journey, examining the film's treatment of his underdog story, Mark Wahlberg's portrayal of the protagonist, and the broader themes of perseverance, resilience, and the allure of the American dream.

Introduction: The Allure of the Underdog Story

The Underdog Paradigm in Sports Cinema: Underdog stories have long held a special place in sports cinema, captivating audiences with the journey of individuals overcoming seemingly insurmountable odds. "Invincible" aligns itself with this narrative tradition, offering a real-life underdog story that resonates beyond the realm of sports. This introduction sets the stage for an exploration of Vince Papale's improbable NFL dream and its cinematic depiction.

Vince Papale: The Man Behind the Legend

Introducing Vince Papale: Before delving into the film's portrayal, this section provides a brief introduction to the real Vince Papale. From his early life and experiences to his journey into professional football, understanding the man behind the legend adds depth to the cinematic narrative. This exploration sets the groundwork for analyzing how "Invincible" translates Papale's life into a compelling on-screen story.

Challenges and Circumstances: Vince Papale's journey is rooted in challenges and circumstances that extend beyond the football field. This part of the chapter examines the real-life hurdles Papale faced, from personal struggles to the economic challenges of working-class Philadelphia. Understanding the context of Papale's life provides insights into the broader themes of the film.

Mark Wahlberg's Portrayal of Vince Papale

Mark Wahlberg's Transformation: Central to the film's success is Mark Wahlberg's portrayal of Vince Papale. This section explores Wahlberg's transformative performance, delving into the actor's physical preparation, character study, and the nuances he brings to the role. Wahlberg's ability to embody Papale becomes a key element in the cinematic translation of the underdog narrative.

Capturing Papale's Spirit: Beyond physical resemblance, Wahlberg aims to capture the spirit and essence of Vince Papale. This exploration dives into how Wahlberg infuses authenticity into his portrayal, tapping into the emotions, motivations, and resilience that defined Papale's real-life journey. The actor's commitment to capturing the character's emotional depth contributes to the film's impact.

The Cinematic Journey: From Bar to Field

Setting the Stage: "Invincible" unfolds against the backdrop of 1970s Philadelphia, a city grappling with economic challenges and a football team in need of revitalization. This section examines how the film sets the stage for Papale's journey, creating a cinematic landscape that mirrors the real-world circumstances that shaped his improbable NFL dream.

Trials and Tribulations: Papale's path from a bartender to a professional football player is marked by trials and tribulations. The film navigates the challenges he faces, both on and off the field, as he confronts skepticism, personal setbacks, and the rigorous demands of professional sports. This part of the chapter analyzes how the film balances the triumphant moments with the struggles inherent in Papale's journey.

The NFL Tryout: Cinematic Tension and Triumph

Building Cinematic Tension: A pivotal moment in the film is Papale's decision to attend an open tryout for the Philadelphia Eagles. This section explores how the film builds cinematic tension around this crucial event, leveraging sports drama conventions to create anticipation and suspense. The tryout becomes a cinematic focal point that encapsulates the underdog narrative.

Triumphant Cinematic Moments: As Papale defies the odds and earns a spot on the Eagles' roster, the film delivers triumphant cinematic moments. This exploration delves into the emotional impact of Papale's success, examining how the film leverages storytelling and visual techniques to celebrate the culmination of his improbable NFL dream. The triumph becomes a cathartic release for both the character and the audience.

Beyond the Field: Personal Growth and Relationships

Personal Growth Arc: "Invincible" goes beyond the football field, portraying Papale's personal growth and transformation. This section analyzes how the film navigates Papale's evolution as an individual, from a man facing adversity to a professional athlete. The character arc becomes a central component in the film's exploration of resilience and the pursuit of dreams.

Relationship Dynamics: The film also delves into Papale's relationships, including his connection with Janet Cantwell, portrayed by Elizabeth Banks. This part of the chapter examines how the film navigates the romantic subplot, adding emotional depth to Papale's journey and highlighting the interpersonal dynamics that contribute to the overall narrative.

Cinematic Techniques: From Soundtrack to Visuals

Soundtrack and Emotional Resonance: The film's soundtrack, composed by Mark Isham, plays a significant role in enhancing emotional resonance. This section explores how the musical score contributes to the overall cinematic experience, underscoring the highs and lows of Papale's journey and eliciting an emotional response from the audience.

Visual Aesthetics and Period Authenticity: "Invincible" employs visual aesthetics that evoke the 1970s, from costume design to cinematography. This exploration delves into how the film achieves period authenticity, immersing audiences in the cultural and visual landscape of the time. The cinematic techniques contribute to the film's ability to transport viewers to the era of Papale's remarkable journey.

Themes of Perseverance, Resilience, and the American Dream

Perseverance as a Driving Force: At its core, "Invincible" explores themes of perseverance and resilience. This section examines how the film positions these qualities as driving forces in Papale's journey, emphasizing the determination that propels him forward despite formidable challenges. The exploration delves into the broader significance of perseverance as a thematic thread.

The American Dream Narrative: Papale's story aligns with the quintessential American dream narrative—the idea that hard work, determination, and opportunity can lead to success. This part of the chapter explores how the film taps into this narrative tradition, presenting Papale's journey as a reflection of the broader cultural ethos surrounding the pursuit of dreams and aspirations.

Conclusion: The Cinematic Triumph of an Underdog

In conclusion, "Invincible" successfully translates Vince Papale's improbable NFL dream into a cinematic triumph of the underdog. From Mark Wahlberg's transformative portrayal to the film's exploration of personal growth, relationship dynamics, and thematic depth, "Invincible" stands as a compelling sports drama that resonates with audiences beyond the realm of football. The chapter underscores the enduring allure of underdog stories and the cinematic power of narratives that celebrate perseverance, resilience, and the realization of extraordinary dreams.

## Mark Wahlberg Anchors Disney Sports Drama

"Invincible" (2006) emerges as a captivating Disney sports drama that brings to life the remarkable journey of Vince Papale. At the heart of the film's success is Mark Wahlberg's transformative performance, anchoring the narrative with emotional depth and authenticity. This chapter explores how Wahlberg embodies the spirit of Vince Papale, navigating the challenges of an underdog narrative within the framework of a Disney sports drama.

Introduction: The Marriage of Disney and Sports Drama

Disney's Legacy in Sports Cinema: Disney has a storied legacy in sports cinema, with a tradition of producing inspirational narratives that celebrate perseverance, triumph over adversity, and the pursuit of dreams. This introduction sets the stage for an exploration of how "Invincible" fits into this cinematic tradition, marrying Disney's storytelling ethos with the compelling sports drama of Vince Papale.

Mark Wahlberg: The Actor and the Underdog

Mark Wahlberg's Rise to Fame: Before delving into his role as Vince Papale, this section provides a brief overview of Mark Wahlberg's career and his rise to fame. From his early days as a musician and underwear model to his transition into acting, Wahlberg's journey becomes a backdrop for understanding the actor who would later anchor "Invincible."

Wahlberg's Affinity for Underdog Roles: Wahlberg has a penchant for underdog roles, often portraying characters facing challenges and adversity. This exploration analyzes Wahlberg's filmography, highlighting roles that align with the underdog narrative and examining how these characters contribute to his reputation as an actor who excels in capturing resilience and determination.

Transformative Performances: Becoming Vince Papale

Physical Transformation: A crucial aspect of Wahlberg's performance as Vince Papale is his physical transformation. This section delves into the actor's commitment to embodying Papale's athletic prowess, exploring the training regimen, physical preparation, and the dedication required to authentically portray a professional football player.

Capturing Papale's Essence: Wahlberg goes beyond a mere physical resemblance, aiming to capture the essence of Vince Papale. This part of the chapter examines how the actor delves into the emotional depth of the character, studying Papale's personality, motivations, and resilience. Wahlberg's ability to tap into the spirit of Papale contributes to the film's emotional resonance.

Authenticity and Emotional Resonance

Balancing Toughness and Vulnerability: Wahlberg navigates the delicate balance between portraying Papale's toughness on the football field and vulnerability in the face of personal challenges. This section explores how the actor brings authenticity to the character, allowing audiences to connect with the human elements of Papale's journey beyond the sports hero persona.

Chemistry with Co-Stars: The success of Wahlberg's performance is also influenced by his chemistry with co-stars, including Elizabeth Banks and Greg Kinnear. This exploration delves into the dynamics between the actors, analyzing how their on-screen interactions contribute to the film's emotional and relational depth.

Navigating the Underdog Narrative: Challenges and Triumphs

Embodying the Underdog Mentality: Wahlberg immerses himself in the underdog mentality that defines Papale's journey. This section examines how the actor captures the nuances of the underdog narrative, portraying the character's determination, resilience, and the internal and external challenges that define the journey from bartender to NFL player.

Cinematic Triumphs: The film strategically leverages Wahlberg's ability to convey triumph over adversity. This part of the chapter analyzes key cinematic moments where Wahlberg's performance elevates the narrative, from Papale's initial struggles to his triumphant realization of making the Eagles' roster. Wahlberg's nuanced portrayal contributes to the emotional impact of these pivotal scenes.

Disney's Touch: Uplifting Narratives and Family-Friendly Appeal

Disney's Sports Drama Formula: Disney has a distinct formula for sports dramas, characterized by uplifting narratives, family-friendly appeal, and a focus on universal themes. This exploration delves into how "Invincible" aligns with the Disney sports drama formula, balancing the inspirational elements of Papale's story with the studio's commitment to creating content suitable for a broad audience.

Impact on Disney's Sports Catalog: "Invincible" adds to Disney's sports catalog, contributing to the studio's reputation for delivering inspirational sports narratives. This section examines the film's place within Disney's broader cinematic landscape, considering its impact on the studio's legacy in sports cinema and its continued resonance with audiences.

Reception and Critical Acclaim

Audience Reception: Wahlberg's performance, coupled with the Disney sports drama formula, resonates with audiences seeking inspirational narratives. This exploration analyzes the reception of "Invincible" among viewers, considering how the film's blend of sports drama and underdog triumph aligns with audience expectations.

Critical Acclaim and Wahlberg's Recognition: The film received positive reviews, and Wahlberg's performance was praised for its authenticity and emotional resonance. This part of the chapter delves into critical acclaim for both the film and Wahlberg's portrayal, exploring how the actor's work in "Invincible" contributed to his recognition within the industry.

Legacy and Continued Impact

Enduring Appeal: "Invincible" continues to have enduring appeal, attracting new audiences and maintaining a place in the cultural conversation. This section examines the factors that contribute to the film's lasting impact, considering its replay value, thematic resonance, and the timeless quality of the underdog narrative.

Wahlberg's Career Trajectory: The success of "Invincible" played a role in shaping Mark Wahlberg's career trajectory. This exploration looks at how the film influenced Wahlberg's subsequent roles, the trajectory of his acting career, and his continued exploration of characters with underdog narratives.

Conclusion: Wahlberg's Anchoring Presence

In conclusion, Mark Wahlberg's anchoring presence is integral to the success of "Invincible" as a Disney sports drama. From his physical transformation to his nuanced portrayal of Vince Papale, Wahlberg contributes to the film's emotional resonance and authenticity. The chapter underscores the actor's ability to navigate the complexities of the underdog narrative within the context of a family-friendly sports drama, cementing "Invincible" as a notable entry in both Disney's cinematic catalog and Wahlberg's career.

## Lean and Formulaic Retelling of Real-Life Miracle Season

"Invincible" (2006) unfolds as a cinematic portrayal of Vince Papale's extraordinary journey, blending elements of inspiration, sports drama, and the classic American underdog narrative. This chapter delves into the film's approach to recounting the real-life miracle season, examining its lean and formulaic storytelling choices, narrative structure, and how these elements contribute to the overall cinematic experience.

Introduction: Crafting a Cinematic Miracle

The Allure of Real-Life Miracle Stories: Before delving into the specifics of "Invincible," this section explores the broader appeal of real-life miracle stories in cinema. From sports triumphs to personal achievements, audiences are drawn to narratives that celebrate the extraordinary against all odds. "Invincible" positions itself within this cinematic tradition, promising a lean and formulaic retelling of Vince Papale's remarkable journey.

Setting the Stage: 1970s Philadelphia

Historical Context and Cultural Landscape: "Invincible" unfolds against the backdrop of 1970s Philadelphia, a city grappling with economic challenges and a football team in need of revitalization. This section examines how the film establishes the historical context and cultural landscape, immersing audiences in the socio-economic conditions that shape Papale's underdog narrative.

Cinematic Choices: Visual Aesthetics and Period Authenticity: The film employs visual aesthetics that evoke the

1970s, from costume design to cinematography. This exploration delves into how the film achieves period authenticity, immersing viewers in the cultural and visual landscape of the time. Cinematic choices contribute to the film's ability to transport audiences to the era of Papale's remarkable journey.

Lean Storytelling: Navigating Papale's Journey

Efficiency in Narrative Choices: "Invincible" adopts a lean storytelling approach, efficiently navigating through the key phases of Vince Papale's journey. This section analyzes how the film makes narrative choices that streamline the storytelling process, focusing on essential events and character developments while omitting extraneous details. The efficiency contributes to the film's pace and rhythm.

Strategic Use of Montages: Montages play a strategic role in conveying the passage of time and the progression of Papale's journey. This part of the chapter examines how the film utilizes montages to encapsulate significant moments, from Papale's training to the Eagles' games. The strategic use of montages allows the film to cover expansive timelines within a condensed cinematic framework.

Formulaic Elements: From Tryouts to Triumphs

Papale's NFL Tryout: Cinematic Tension and Triumph: A pivotal moment in the film is Papale's decision to attend an open tryout for the Philadelphia Eagles. This section explores how the film builds cinematic tension around this crucial event, leveraging sports drama conventions to create anticipation and suspense. The tryout becomes a cinematic focal point that encapsulates the underdog narrative.

Triumphant Cinematic Moments: As Papale defies the odds and earns a spot on the Eagles' roster, the film delivers triumphant cinematic moments. This exploration delves into the emotional impact of Papale's success, examining how the film leverages storytelling and visual techniques to celebrate the culmination of his improbable NFL dream. The triumph becomes a cathartic release for both the character and the audience.

Character Dynamics: Papale and Supporting Cast

Janet Cantwell's Role: Beyond Papale, the film introduces supporting characters, including Janet Cantwell, portrayed by Elizabeth Banks. This section examines the dynamics between Papale and Cantwell, delving into how the film navigates the romantic subplot and adds emotional depth to Papale's journey. Character dynamics contribute to the broader narrative and thematic elements.

Interactions with Teammates and Coaches: Papale's interactions with teammates and coaches become integral to the film's portrayal of camaraderie and mentorship. This exploration analyzes how the film establishes relationships within the Eagles' team, from initial skepticism to eventual camaraderie. The dynamics contribute to the sense of community and teamwork inherent in sports narratives.

Challenges and Triumphs: A Cinematic Balancing Act

Cinematic Triumphs Amidst Struggles: "Invincible" strategically balances challenges and triumphs within its narrative framework. This section examines how the film navigates Papale's struggles, both on and off the field, juxtaposed with moments of triumph. The cinematic balancing act contributes to the emotional depth of the narrative, keeping audiences engaged with Papale's journey.

Lean Approach to Personal Struggles: While the film touches on Papale's personal struggles, it adopts a lean approach to these elements of the narrative. This exploration delves into how the film addresses personal challenges without delving too deeply into extraneous details, maintaining focus on the central underdog narrative. The lean approach contributes to the film's streamlined storytelling.

Disney's Influence: Uplift and Family-Friendly Appeal

Disney's Sports Drama Formula: Disney has a distinct formula for sports dramas, characterized by uplifting narratives, family-friendly appeal, and a focus on universal themes. This exploration delves into how "Invincible" aligns with the Disney sports drama formula, balancing the inspirational elements of Papale's story with the studio's commitment to creating content suitable for a broad audience.

Impact on Narrative Choices: Disney's influence is evident in the film's narrative choices, emphasizing uplifting moments and an overall positive tone. This section analyzes how the influence of Disney's storytelling ethos shapes the film's approach to Papale's journey, contributing to its family-friendly appeal and the enduring resonance of the underdog narrative.

Critical Reception: Successes and Criticisms

Audience Reception: "Invincible" found success among audiences seeking inspirational narratives. This exploration analyzes the reception of the film, considering how its lean and formulaic approach resonated with viewers seeking a classic underdog story within the context of a Disney sports drama.

Criticisms and Limitations: Despite its successes, the film faced criticisms for its formulaic elements and predictable narrative arc. This section examines the limitations of "Invincible," addressing the criticisms leveled against its lean storytelling choices and formulaic approach. The analysis considers how these aspects may impact the film's reception among certain audiences.

Conclusion: A Cinematic Miracle in Lean Proportions

In conclusion, "Invincible" crafts a cinematic miracle within lean proportions, embracing a formulaic approach to recount Vince Papale's real-life miracle season. The film strategically navigates through Papale's journey, utilizing efficiency in storytelling, formulaic elements, and Disney's influence to deliver a family-friendly sports drama with enduring appeal. The chapter underscores how the lean and formulaic choices contribute to the film's success as a classic underdog narrative within the realm of sports cinema.

### Philadelphia Eagles' Claim to Underdog Lore

"Invincible" (2006) not only tells the remarkable story of Vince Papale but also weaves itself into the broader narrative of the Philadelphia Eagles. This chapter explores how the film contributes to the Eagles' claim to underdog lore, examining the symbiotic relationship between the team's history and the cinematic portrayal of Papale's improbable journey.

Introduction: The Eagles and Their Underdog Identity

Philadelphia Eagles: A Franchise with a Legacy: Before delving into the specifics of "Invincible," this section provides an overview of the Philadelphia Eagles' historical context within the NFL. From early struggles to moments of triumph, the Eagles' journey sets the stage for understanding the underdog identity that becomes intertwined with the franchise.

The Underdog Mentality: The Eagles have embraced the underdog mentality, representing resilience in the face of challenges. This exploration delves into the cultural and sporting significance of the underdog identity, examining how it has become an integral part of the Eagles' narrative and fan culture.

Vince Papale and the Eagles: A Symbiotic Relationship

Papale's Impact on Team Dynamics: "Invincible" introduces Vince Papale as a pivotal figure in the Eagles' history. This section explores how Papale's journey, as depicted in the film, impacted the dynamics within the Eagles' team. From initial skepticism to camaraderie, Papale's presence becomes a catalyst for a transformative season.

Team's Impact on Papale's Journey: Reciprocally, the Eagles play a crucial role in shaping Papale's journey. This part of the chapter examines how the team becomes a supporting character in the film, influencing Papale's growth, resilience, and ultimate triumph. The symbiotic relationship between Papale and the Eagles is central to the underdog narrative.

Cinematic Recreation of Eagles' History

Historical Accuracy vs. Cinematic Interpretation: "Invincible" navigates the delicate balance between historical accuracy and cinematic interpretation. This section analyzes how the film recreates key moments in Eagles' history, from Papale's tryout to pivotal games, and the liberties taken to enhance the cinematic narrative. The recreation contributes to the Eagles' claim to underdog lore within the context of the film.

Visualizing Eagles' Triumphs and Struggles: Cinematography plays a crucial role in visualizing the Eagles' triumphs and struggles. This exploration delves into how the film uses visual elements to capture iconic moments in Eagles' history, emphasizing the team's underdog identity. From on-field action to emotional reactions, the visual storytelling enhances the Eagles' claim to underdog lore.

Underdog Narratives: Team and Individual Perspectives

Team Underdog Narrative: The Eagles' underdog narrative extends beyond individual players to encompass the entire team. This section examines how "Invincible" reinforces the team's collective underdog identity, portraying the Eagles as a resilient unit facing challenges and defying expectations. The film's narrative choices contribute to the team's claim to underdog lore.

Papale's Individual Underdog Journey: While the team embodies the underdog spirit, Papale's individual journey becomes a microcosm of the larger narrative. This part of the chapter explores how the film focuses on Papale as the quintessential underdog, emphasizing his personal struggles, triumphs, and the transformative impact he has on the team. Papale's story adds nuance to the Eagles' underdog identity.

Impact on Fan Culture and Identity

Fan Connection to Underdog Lore: The Eagles' underdog lore is not confined to the field but extends to the fanbase. This exploration delves into how "Invincible" strengthens the connection between the team and its fans, solidifying the underdog identity as a unifying force. The film becomes a cultural touchstone that resonates with Eagles' enthusiasts, fostering a shared identity rooted in resilience.

Legacy of Underdog Symbolism: The impact of "Invincible" on the Eagles' underdog symbolism extends beyond the film's release. This section examines how the legacy of the underdog narrative, as depicted in the film, continues to influence the Eagles' cultural identity. The symbolism becomes a rallying point for fans, ingrained in the team's legacy and celebrated in moments of triumph.

Cultural Significance: From Film to Franchise

Elevating the Eagles' Cultural Relevance: "Invincible" elevates the Eagles' cultural relevance, contributing to the team's broader narrative in popular culture. This exploration analyzes how the film's success intersects with the Eagles' journey on the field, amplifying the team's cultural significance and resonating with audiences beyond traditional sports enthusiasts.

Beyond the NFL: Impact on Philadelphia's Identity: The Eagles' underdog narrative, as portrayed in "Invincible," extends its impact beyond the NFL. This part of the chapter explores how the film contributes to Philadelphia's identity, becoming a symbol of the city's resilience and the embodiment of the underdog spirit that permeates various facets of Philadelphia's cultural landscape.

Critical Reception: Authenticity vs. Cinematic Liberty

Authenticity and Fan Approval: While the film received praise for capturing the underdog spirit of the Eagles, there were discussions about the balance between authenticity and cinematic liberty. This section delves into how fans and critics responded to the film's portrayal of the Eagles' history, assessing the authenticity of the underdog narrative and its reception among the Eagles' faithful.

Acknowledging Cinematic License: "Invincible" acknowledges its cinematic license in recreating historical events. This exploration discusses how the film addresses the inherent challenges of adapting real-life stories for the screen, balancing the need for authenticity with the creative liberties taken to enhance the cinematic experience. The acknowledgment of cinematic license becomes a crucial aspect of the film's reception.

Conclusion: Eagles' Underdog Lore in Cinematic Glory

In conclusion, "Invincible" contributes to the Philadelphia Eagles' claim to underdog lore in cinematic glory. The film intertwines the team's historical underdog identity with Vince Papale's individual journey, creating a symbiotic relationship that resonates with fans and enhances the Eagles' cultural significance. The chapter underscores how "Invincible" becomes a cinematic celebration of the Eagles' underdog spirit, elevating the team's narrative to iconic status within the realm of sports cinema.

## Chapter 9: Jerry Maguire (1996)
## Show Me the Money: The Origins of a Modern Catchphrase

"Jerry Maguire" (1996) not only left an indelible mark on sports cinema but also introduced a catchphrase that transcended the film itself. This chapter explores the origins of the iconic phrase "Show me the money," its cultural impact, and how it became a lasting symbol of the film's influence on language, popular culture, and the business of sports.

Introduction: A Catchphrase That Resonates

The Power of Catchphrases: Before delving into the specifics of "Jerry Maguire," this section reflects on the cultural significance of catchphrases. From movie lines to slogans, catchphrases have the power to permeate society, becoming linguistic touchstones that evoke memories, emotions, and the essence of the cultural moment. "Show me the money" is one such catchphrase that emerged from the world of sports cinema.

Contextualizing "Show Me the Money": This exploration provides context to the catchphrase, situating it within the narrative of "Jerry Maguire" and the character dynamics between Jerry Maguire, played by Tom Cruise, and Rod Tidwell, portrayed by Cuba Gooding Jr. The catchphrase becomes a pivotal moment in the film, encapsulating themes of ambition, negotiation, and the commodification of sports.

The Birth of "Show Me the Money" in Cinematic Context

Narrative Context: Jerry and Rod's Dynamic: "Jerry Maguire" revolves around the eponymous sports agent's journey of moral reckoning and professional redemption. This section analyzes the narrative context in which the catchphrase is born, exploring the dynamic between Jerry Maguire and his client Rod Tidwell. The catchphrase emerges as a declaration of financial validation within the context of their tumultuous relationship.

Cinematic Impact: Scene Analysis: The film's most memorable scene featuring the catchphrase is dissected in this part of the chapter. The analysis delves into the nuances of the dialogue, the emotional crescendo it represents, and the chemistry between Cruise and Gooding Jr. Cinematic choices, such as delivery, timing, and visual cues, contribute to the catchphrase's resonance beyond the screen.

Transcending the Screen: "Show Me the Money" Goes Viral

Popularity Beyond the Film: "Jerry Maguire" achieved widespread success, and with it, the catchphrase "Show me the money" transcended the boundaries of the film itself. This section explores how the catchphrase gained a life of its own, extending its popularity to everyday conversations, parodies, and references across various forms of media.

Impact on Sports Culture: Athletes and Contracts: The catchphrase found a natural home within sports culture, mirroring the themes of negotiation and financial validation depicted in the film. Athletes began incorporating "Show me the money" into contract negotiations, interviews, and victory celebrations. This exploration delves into how the catchphrase became a symbolic demand for recognition and reward in the world of sports.

Linguistic Evolution: "Show Me the Money" in Everyday Language

Incorporation into Everyday Language: The catchphrase underwent linguistic evolution, seamlessly integrating into everyday language. This part of the chapter investigates how "Show me the money" transitioned from a movie line to a versatile expression used in various contexts beyond sports and business. Its adaptability contributed to its enduring presence in colloquial discourse.

Cultural References and Parodies: "Show me the money" became a source of inspiration for cultural references and parodies across different mediums. From television shows to commercials, its ubiquity reinforced its status as a cultural touchstone. The chapter explores notable instances of the catchphrase's appearance in popular culture, showcasing its versatility and enduring relevance.

Business and Marketing Impact: Capitalizing on the Catchphrase

Marketing and Branding: Recognizing the catchphrase's cultural capital, marketers and brands capitalized on its popularity. This section examines how "Show me the money" became a marketing tool, featured in advertising campaigns, merchandise, and promotional materials. The catchphrase's association with financial success made it a powerful tool for selling products and services.

Legacy in Advertising: The catchphrase's legacy extended to the advertising industry, where it was repurposed to convey messages about value, quality, and the promise of a lucrative deal. This exploration delves into how advertisers leveraged the catchphrase to capture consumer attention and communicate the idea of getting the best possible outcome.

Challenges and Criticisms: The Catchphrase's Double-Edged Sword

Overuse and Parody: As with any widely adopted catchphrase, "Show me the money" faced challenges related to overuse and parody. This part of the chapter acknowledges the criticisms leveled against the catchphrase, including accusations of it becoming clichéd or losing its original impact through repetition and imitation.

Decontextualization: The catchphrase's journey beyond the film also led to instances of decontextualization. This exploration examines how the catchphrase, when divorced from its original narrative and emotional resonance, risked losing the depth of meaning that characterized its pivotal moment in "Jerry Maguire."

The Catchphrase's Cultural Endurance: A Linguistic Legacy

Enduring Impact: Despite challenges, "Show me the money" has endured as a linguistic legacy of "Jerry Maguire." This section explores the catchphrase's lasting impact, reflecting on its continued resonance in contemporary language, its entry into lexicons of popular expressions, and its ability to evoke nostalgia for the film and the era in which it originated.

Contributions to Language: Beyond its role as a catchphrase, "Show me the money" contributed idiomatic expressions to the English language. This part of the chapter delves into how the catchphrase influenced language use, with its structure and sentiment being repurposed in various linguistic forms to convey a desire for proof, validation, or tangible results.

Conclusion: "Show Me the Money" as a Cultural Touchstone

In conclusion, "Jerry Maguire" gave birth to more than a cinematic catchphrase—it created a cultural touchstone. "Show me the money" transcended the screen, becoming a symbol of ambition, financial validation, and the intersection of sports, entertainment, and business. This chapter highlights the catchphrase's origins, its cultural impact, and its enduring legacy as a linguistic phenomenon that continues to resonate in contemporary discourse.

## Tom Cruise at His Charismatic Peak

"Jerry Maguire" not only marked a significant point in sports cinema but also showcased Tom Cruise at the height of his charismatic prowess. This chapter delves into Cruise's portrayal of Jerry Maguire, examining how his performance contributed to the film's success, its impact on his career, and the enduring legacy of his charismatic peak in this iconic role.

Introduction: Tom Cruise and the Role of Jerry Maguire

The Cruise Factor: Before delving into Cruise's portrayal, this section reflects on Tom Cruise's standing in Hollywood during the mid-1990s. Cruise was already a megastar known for his charm, versatility, and box office appeal. "Jerry Maguire" provided him with a role that not only showcased his acting range but also allowed him to explore the complexities of a character navigating moral dilemmas in the cutthroat world of sports management.

Jerry Maguire: A Departure for Cruise: This exploration sets the stage by discussing how Jerry Maguire represented a departure from Cruise's previous roles. Unlike the action-oriented characters he was known for, Jerry Maguire was a sports agent dealing with ethical conflicts, providing Cruise with an opportunity to showcase a different facet of his acting abilities.

Cruise's Jerry Maguire: Balancing Charisma and Vulnerability

Charismatic Charm: One of Cruise's defining characteristics is his charismatic charm, and in "Jerry Maguire," this quality takes center stage. This section analyzes how Cruise infuses Jerry Maguire with an undeniable charm, making the character likable even as he grapples with moral quandaries. Cruise's charisma becomes a vital component in establishing audience connection and empathy.

Vulnerability and Complexity: While Cruise's charisma is a standout feature, his portrayal goes beyond surface charm. This part of the chapter explores how Cruise injects vulnerability and complexity into Jerry Maguire. As the character faces professional challenges, ethical dilemmas, and personal growth, Cruise's nuanced performance elevates Jerry Maguire from a typical leading man to a multi-dimensional protagonist.

The Journey of Jerry Maguire: Cruise's Character Arc

Professional Rise and Fall: Cruise's performance is examined in the context of Jerry Maguire's character arc. From the zenith of success as a high-powered sports agent to the moral awakening that leads to professional downfall, Cruise navigates the complexities of Jerry's journey with conviction. The analysis delves into how Cruise's portrayal captures the highs and lows of the character's professional life.

Romantic Dynamics: Chemistry with Renée Zellweger: Jerry Maguire's romantic subplot is a pivotal aspect of the film, and Cruise's on-screen chemistry with Renée Zellweger, who plays Dorothy Boyd, is crucial to its success. This section explores how Cruise's interactions with Zellweger contribute to the authenticity of the romantic narrative, showcasing a different dimension of Cruise's acting abilities in the realm of interpersonal dynamics.

Cruise's Collaboration with Cameron Crowe: Director-Actor Synergy

Crowe and Cruise: A Dynamic Duo: The synergy between Cruise and director Cameron Crowe is central to the success of "Jerry Maguire." This exploration delves into the collaborative relationship between the actor and director, examining how Crowe's nuanced storytelling and Cruise's performance complement each other. The chapter highlights how Crowe's directorial choices enhance Cruise's portrayal, creating a seamless fusion of character and narrative.

Impact of Collaborative Choices: From memorable scenes to character nuances, this part of the chapter analyzes specific collaborative choices that shaped Cruise's performance. It explores how Crowe's direction influenced Cruise's character choices, contributing to the authenticity of Jerry Maguire's emotional journey and the overall impact of Cruise's charismatic peak in the film.

Critical Acclaim: Cruise's Performance and Awards Recognition

Critical Reception: "Jerry Maguire" received critical acclaim, and Cruise's performance was a standout element. This section explores how critics responded to Cruise's portrayal, acknowledging the depth he brought to the character. The analysis delves into specific aspects of Cruise's performance that garnered praise, from his delivery of iconic lines to his ability to convey internal conflict.

Awards Recognition: Oscar Nomination: Cruise's performance in "Jerry Maguire" earned him an Academy Award nomination for Best Actor. This part of the chapter examines the significance of the nomination, considering how it reflected industry acknowledgment of Cruise's ability to excel in roles that demanded emotional depth and complexity.

Impact on Cruise's Career: Evolving Beyond Action Roles

Career Transition: "Jerry Maguire" marked a pivotal moment in Cruise's career, signaling a transition beyond the action roles that had defined much of his earlier filmography. This section explores how the success of the film contributed to Cruise's evolving reputation as an actor capable of tackling diverse roles that demanded more than physical prowess.

Legacy of Versatility: The legacy of Cruise's performance in "Jerry Maguire" extends to his subsequent filmography. This exploration delves into how the film opened doors for Cruise to take on a wider range of roles, showcasing his versatility as an actor beyond the action-hero archetype. The chapter reflects on how "Jerry Maguire" served as a catalyst for Cruise's evolving career trajectory.

Cruise's Charismatic Peak: Beyond "Jerry Maguire"

Subsequent Roles and Charismatic Continuity: Cruise's charismatic peak in "Jerry Maguire" wasn't an isolated event. This part of the chapter examines how Cruise's subsequent roles continued to leverage his charismatic charm, demonstrating that "Jerry Maguire" was a watershed moment in his career that paved the way for a sustained period of success and versatility.

Cultural Impact: Popularity and Enduring Appeal: The cultural impact of Cruise's charismatic peak is discussed in terms of the enduring appeal of "Jerry Maguire." This exploration considers how the film, anchored by Cruise's performance, continues to resonate with audiences, maintaining its status as a classic that represents a specific moment in both sports and cinematic history.

Conclusion: Cruise's Charismatic Legacy in "Jerry Maguire"

In conclusion, Tom Cruise's portrayal of Jerry Maguire stands as a testament to his charismatic peak—a moment when his acting abilities transcended traditional action roles. Cruise brought depth, vulnerability, and charm to the character, contributing to the film's critical and commercial success. This chapter underscores how "Jerry Maguire" marked a defining moment in Cruise's career, showcasing his ability to evolve beyond established archetypes and embrace a diverse range of roles, solidifying his status as one of Hollywood's enduring leading men.

### Dramedy Balance Earns Widespread Appeal

In the landscape of sports cinema, "Jerry Maguire" (1996) stands out not only for its exploration of the cutthroat world of sports management but also for its unique blend of drama and comedy—a delicate balance that contributed to the film's widespread appeal. This chapter delves into the intricacies of the dramady genre within "Jerry Maguire," exploring how director Cameron Crowe masterfully interweaves humor and poignant moments to create a film that resonates with a broad audience.

Introduction: The Art of Blending Drama and Comedy

Defining Dramedy in Cinema: Before delving into the specific dramady elements of "Jerry Maguire," this section provides a contextual overview of the dramady genre in cinema. It explores how dramadies navigate the complex terrain between drama and comedy, aiming to evoke both emotional depth and laughter. "Jerry Maguire" emerges as a notable example of this genre fusion, and the chapter sets out to dissect the components that contribute to its successful balance.

The Unique Appeal of Dramedies: The exploration continues by discussing the unique appeal of dramadies to audiences. It examines how the combination of humor and heartfelt moments creates a cinematic experience that resonates with a diverse range of viewers, allowing them to engage with the characters and narrative on multiple emotional levels.

Crafting Comedy in the World of Sports Management

Setting the Tone: Opening Scene Analysis: The chapter kicks off with an analysis of the film's opening scene, dissecting how Crowe sets the tone for the dramady to unfold. The examination delves into the use of humor to introduce the fast-paced and often absurd world of sports management. From Jerry Maguire's frenetic monologue to comedic glimpses of the sports agency, the opening scene establishes a comedic foundation that runs throughout the film.

Comic Relief Characters: Jay Mohr's Bob Sugar: This section explores the role of supporting characters in providing comic relief. Jay Mohr's portrayal of Bob Sugar, Jerry Maguire's ambitious and conniving colleague, adds a layer of humor to the narrative. The analysis delves into specific scenes and interactions that highlight Mohr's comedic timing and the character's contribution to the film's lighter moments.

Navigating Ethical Dilemmas with Humor and Heart

Ethical Quandaries as Comedy: Jerry's Mission Statement: The film's central ethical dilemma, embodied in Jerry Maguire's mission statement, is examined through the lens of comedy. This part of the chapter analyzes how Crowe uses humor to navigate Jerry's bold but precarious move to redefine his professional values. The mission statement scene becomes a pivotal moment of comedy, injecting levity into the film's exploration of morality in sports management.

Rod Tidwell: Cuba Gooding Jr.'s Comedic Prowess: Cuba Gooding Jr.'s portrayal of Rod Tidwell, the flamboyant and outspoken football player, is a comedic tour de force. This exploration delves into specific scenes that showcase Gooding

Jr.'s comedic prowess, emphasizing how the character of Rod contributes to the film's humor while also serving as a catalyst for emotional depth.

Emotional Resonance Amidst Laughter

Romantic Dynamics: Renée Zellweger's Dorothy Boyd: The dramady balance extends to the romantic subplot involving Jerry Maguire and Renée Zellweger's character, Dorothy Boyd. This section explores how Crowe weaves elements of romance into the narrative, infusing humor into the evolving relationship between Jerry and Dorothy. The examination considers the film's portrayal of love and relationships as both poignant and comedic.

Jonathan Lipnicki's Ray Boyd: Family Dynamics: Family dynamics, particularly the relationship between Jerry and Ray Boyd, Jerry's young client, contribute to the film's emotional resonance. This analysis focuses on specific scenes involving Jonathan Lipnicki's character, exploring how the father-son dynamic is portrayed with humor and heart. Lipnicki's charismatic performance adds a layer of innocence and humor to the film's emotional core.

Balancing Act: Handling Serious Themes with Humor

Sports Industry Critique: The Humor in Satire: "Jerry Maguire" serves as a satire of the sports management industry, critiquing its excesses and moral ambiguities. This part of the chapter delves into the film's satirical elements, exploring how Crowe uses humor as a tool for social commentary. The analysis considers specific scenes that satirize the commodification of athletes and the competitive landscape of the sports agency business.

Jerry's Moral Journey: Comedy in Self-Reflection: As Jerry Maguire undergoes a moral transformation, the film employs comedy to navigate his introspective moments. This section analyzes scenes that depict Jerry's self-reflection and the humor embedded in his realization of the consequences of his past actions. The comedic elements serve to lighten the weight of the film's serious themes, making the exploration of morality accessible to a broader audience.

The Soundtrack's Role in Enhancing Dramedy Dynamics

Musical Choices: Tone and Atmosphere: Cameron Crowe is renowned for his adept use of music in film, and "Jerry Maguire" is no exception. This exploration delves into the soundtrack's role in enhancing the dramady dynamics. It analyzes how musical choices contribute to the film's tonal shifts, seamlessly blending comedic and poignant moments. Specific scenes and the corresponding musical accompaniment are dissected to highlight the synergy between music and narrative.

Memorable Musical Moments: "Secret Garden" and Beyond: The chapter explores specific musical moments that exemplify the dramady balance. From Bruce Springsteen's "Secret Garden" to other iconic tracks, the analysis delves into how these musical choices enhance the emotional impact of scenes while also adding an element of humor. The soundtrack becomes an integral part of the film's overall tonal tapestry.

Critical and Audience Reception: A Universal Appeal

Critical Acclaim: Balancing Act Acknowledged: "Jerry Maguire" received widespread critical acclaim, and this section examines how the film's dramady balance was acknowledged by reviewers. Critical perspectives on the seamless fusion of humor and drama are explored, emphasizing how Crowe's directorial choices and the performances of the cast contributed to the film's positive reception.

Audience Appeal: Crossing Demographic Boundaries: The film's appeal extended beyond critics to a diverse audience. This exploration considers how the dramady balance contributed to the film's ability to resonate with viewers across demographic boundaries. From sports enthusiasts to those seeking a heartfelt romantic comedy, "Jerry Maguire" achieved a universal appeal that transcended genre expectations.

Legacy: Inspiring a New Wave of Dramedies

Influence on Subsequent Dramedies: The chapter concludes by reflecting on the legacy of "Jerry Maguire" within the dramady genre. It explores how the film's success influenced subsequent productions, inspiring a new wave of films that sought to replicate the delicate balance between humor and drama. The analysis considers specific examples of films that followed in the footsteps of "Jerry Maguire."

Enduring Popularity: A Film for All Seasons: The enduring popularity of "Jerry Maguire" is attributed to its timeless dramady elements. This section explores why the film continues to be celebrated and revisited, maintaining its status as a film for all seasons that offers audiences a unique blend of laughter and heart.

Conclusion: "Jerry Maguire" as a Pinnacle of Dramady Mastery

In conclusion, "Jerry Maguire" emerges as a pinnacle of dramady mastery within sports cinema. Cameron Crowe's adept direction, coupled with stellar performances, creates a film that seamlessly navigates between humor and heartfelt moments. The dramady balance not only contributed to the film's critical and commercial success but also established "Jerry Maguire" as a timeless classic that continues to resonate with audiences, inspiring a genre-defying approach to storytelling in sports cinema.

## Lasting Cultural Impact Beyond Football

"Jerry Maguire," beyond its portrayal of the cutthroat world of sports management, has left an indelible mark on popular culture that extends far beyond the realm of football. This chapter delves into the film's lasting cultural impact, examining how its memorable quotes, characters, and themes have permeated society, shaping conversations about love, integrity, and the pursuit of genuine happiness.

Introduction: Beyond the Gridiron

Contextualizing Cultural Impact: Before exploring the cultural impact of "Jerry Maguire," this section sets the stage by discussing the film's initial reception and how it transcended its sports-centric narrative. "Jerry Maguire" resonated not only with sports enthusiasts but also with a broader audience, making it a cultural touchstone that continues to be referenced and celebrated.

Defying Genre Conventions: A Film for Every Audience: The chapter begins by examining how "Jerry Maguire" defied genre conventions, positioning itself as a film that transcends the sports drama label. It explores the factors that contributed to the film's universal appeal, making it accessible to viewers who might not typically be drawn to sports-themed narratives.

Quotable Lines: The Lingering Power of Dialogue

"Show Me the Money": A Modern Catchphrase: One of the most iconic catchphrases in cinematic history originated in "Jerry Maguire." This section delves into the origins of the famous line, "Show me the money!" and explores how it became a cultural catchphrase that extends beyond the film. From sports arenas to everyday conversations, the quote has taken on a life of its own, symbolizing the pursuit of success and recognition.

"You Complete Me": Romantic Declarations in Popular Culture: The chapter then turns its attention to another memorable line from the film, "You complete me." This exploration considers how this romantic declaration became synonymous with expressions of love and devotion in popular culture. The analysis delves into the enduring impact of the line, both in cinematic history and as a part of everyday vernacular.

Archetypal Characters: The Jerry Maguire Effect

Jerry Maguire: The Everyman Protagonist: This section examines how the character of Jerry Maguire, portrayed by Tom Cruise, became an archetypal figure representing the struggles and triumphs of the modern professional. From his moral awakening to his journey of self-discovery, Jerry Maguire resonates as an everyman protagonist, making him relatable to a broad audience.

Rod Tidwell: The Unforgettable Sidekick: Cuba Gooding Jr.'s portrayal of Rod Tidwell, the flamboyant football player, contributed to the film's cultural impact. This exploration analyzes how Rod Tidwell became an unforgettable sidekick, challenging stereotypes and showcasing the importance of self-worth and integrity in the face of success.

Cinematic Influences: Paving the Way for Dramedies

Crowe's Directorial Style: Influence on Subsequent Films: The chapter considers the influence of Cameron Crowe's directorial style on subsequent films. Specifically, it explores how "Jerry Maguire" paved the way for a new wave of dramedies that blended humor and heartfelt moments. Crowe's ability to navigate the complexities of human relationships with wit and authenticity set a precedent for filmmakers exploring similar thematic territory.

Dramedy Renaissance: Echoes of "Jerry Maguire" in Contemporary Cinema: The exploration extends to contemporary cinema, identifying films that echo the dramedy sensibilities of "Jerry Maguire." From character-driven narratives to exploration of moral quandaries, the chapter reflects on how the film's legacy is evident in the continued popularity of dramedies in the cinematic landscape.

Soundtrack: A Musical Tapestry of Emotional Resonance

Impact of Musical Choices: Beyond the Silver Screen: Cameron Crowe's curated soundtrack for "Jerry Maguire" not only enhanced the film but also left an enduring impact beyond the silver screen. This section explores how the musical choices became an integral part of the film's cultural legacy, influencing music consumption trends and inspiring nostalgia for a generation.

Continued Popularity of Soundtrack: Enduring Musical Appeal: The chapter delves into the continued popularity of the film's soundtrack, considering how its eclectic mix of songs has maintained its appeal over the years. From classic rock to soulful ballads, the soundtrack's enduring popularity speaks to its ability to evoke emotions and enhance the overall cultural impact of "Jerry Maguire."

Social Commentary: Exploring Themes That Transcend Time

Integrity in Professionalism: Lessons for the Modern Workplace: This exploration delves into the film's social commentary on integrity in the workplace. The analysis considers how the film's portrayal of Jerry Maguire's moral journey resonates with contemporary discussions about ethics, professionalism, and the pursuit of meaningful work.

Modern Relationships: Love, Vulnerability, and Communication: The chapter then turns its attention to the film's exploration of modern relationships. It examines how the romantic dynamics between Jerry and Dorothy Boyd continue to offer insights into love, vulnerability, and effective communication in contemporary relationships. The enduring relevance of these themes contributes to the film's cultural impact.

Parodies and Homages: Keeping "Jerry Maguire" Alive

Parodies in Popular Culture: The impact of "Jerry Maguire" is further explored through parodies that have permeated popular culture. From television shows to comedy sketches, the chapter examines how the film's memorable scenes and characters have been playfully reimagined, keeping the spirit of "Jerry Maguire" alive in the collective imagination.

Homages in Film and Television: A Nod to a Classic: The exploration extends to homages in film and television, where creators pay tribute to the enduring legacy of "Jerry Maguire."

This section considers how the film has become a reference point in popular media, with nods and references that celebrate its contributions to cinematic and cultural history.

Conclusion: "Jerry Maguire" as a Cultural Milestone

In conclusion, "Jerry Maguire" transcends its origins as a sports drama, evolving into a cultural milestone with a lasting impact that reaches far beyond football. The film's quotable lines, archetypal characters, and thematic exploration of love and integrity have embedded it in the cultural consciousness. As a cinematic touchstone, "Jerry Maguire" continues to inspire discussions about relationships, ethics, and the pursuit of personal and professional fulfillment, ensuring its place in the pantheon of enduring cultural classics.

## Chapter 10: Draft Day (2014)
### Pulling Back the Curtain on the NFL Draft

In the realm of sports cinema, "Draft Day" (2014) emerges as a unique exploration of the intense and high-stakes world of the NFL Draft. This chapter delves into the film's portrayal of the NFL Draft, dissecting how it pulls back the curtain on the behind-the-scenes machinations, strategic decisions, and emotional rollercoaster that define one of the most crucial events in professional football.

Introduction: The Drama Behind the Selections

Setting the Stage: The NFL Draft as a Dramatic Canvas: Before delving into the specifics of "Draft Day," this section provides an overview of the significance of the NFL Draft in the world of American football. It outlines the crucial role the draft plays in shaping the future of NFL franchises, building anticipation and excitement among fans, and serving as a platform for emerging talent to make their mark on the professional stage.

Unique Perspective: Fictionalized Drama and Real-Life Tensions: The chapter introduces the film "Draft Day" as a fictionalized drama that offers a unique perspective on the NFL Draft. It explores the intersection of real-life tensions that accompany the draft process with the cinematic liberties taken to create a compelling narrative. The analysis sets the stage for a deep dive into the film's portrayal of the draft and its impact on the characters involved.

The Draft Day Experience: Cinematic Realism and Dramatic License

Authenticity in Portraying the Draft Room: This section delves into the film's efforts to authentically portray the inner workings of an NFL team's draft room. It explores the set design, the strategic discussions, and the overall ambiance created to immerse viewers in the high-pressure environment where crucial decisions are made. The analysis considers the film's balance between cinematic realism and the necessity of taking creative liberties to enhance dramatic tension.

Character Dynamics: The Team Behind the Team: "Draft Day" introduces a cast of characters essential to the drafting process, beyond the players themselves. This exploration focuses on the dynamics among team executives, coaches, scouts, and the general manager, played by Kevin Costner. It analyzes how the film portrays the collaborative efforts and occasional conflicts within this team behind the team, offering a nuanced depiction of the decision-making process.

Strategic Maneuvering: Trades, Picks, and Draft-Day Drama

Trades and Negotiations: Shaping the Team's Destiny: One of the central elements of the film revolves around trades and negotiations during the draft. This section examines how "Draft Day" portrays the strategic maneuvering that occurs as teams jockey for position, make deals, and leverage their picks to secure the best talent. The analysis delves into specific scenes that highlight the negotiation tactics employed by teams, adding an element of suspense to the narrative.

Picks and Predictions: The Unpredictability of the Draft: The unpredictability of the draft is a key theme explored in the film. This part of the chapter dissects how "Draft Day" captures the tension surrounding player selections, the anticipation of draft picks, and the impact of unexpected choices. It considers the film's ability to convey the emotional rollercoaster experienced by both teams and fans as they navigate the unpredictable landscape of the draft.

The Human Element: Players and Personal Stories

Players as Individuals: Beyond the Stats: While "Draft Day" delves into the strategic aspects of the draft, it also places emphasis on the human stories behind the players. This section explores how the film presents players as individuals with personal narratives, aspirations, and challenges. The analysis considers specific character arcs and moments that humanize the athletes, adding depth to their portrayal beyond their statistics and on-field prowess.

Personal Challenges: Balancing Football and Life: The chapter delves into the personal challenges faced by players as they navigate the draft process. From familial expectations to personal aspirations, "Draft Day" explores the intersection of football careers with the broader context of players' lives. This analysis considers how the film balances the intensity of the draft with the human element, creating a multi-layered narrative that resonates with audiences.

Cinematic Techniques: Enhancing the Draft-Day Drama

Cinematography and Pacing: Capturing the Tension: The film's cinematography and pacing play a crucial role in conveying the tension and drama of draft day. This section dissects how cinematic techniques, including camera angles, editing choices, and the use of suspenseful music, contribute to the overall atmosphere of the film. The analysis considers specific scenes where these techniques are employed to heighten the emotional impact of the draft process.

Flashbacks and Exposition: Building Character Backstories: To enhance the narrative, "Draft Day" incorporates flashbacks and exposition to provide insights into characters' histories. This part of the chapter examines how these storytelling devices are utilized to build character backstories, establish motivations, and create a richer understanding of the individuals involved in the draft. The analysis considers the effectiveness of these narrative tools in shaping the overall storytelling experience.

NFL Draft Realism: Balancing Fiction with Reality

Consulting with NFL Experts: Navigating Authenticity: To maintain authenticity, the filmmakers of "Draft Day" consulted with NFL experts during the production process. This section explores how the collaboration with professionals in the football industry influenced the film's portrayal of the draft. The analysis considers the balance between staying true to the real-world intricacies of the NFL Draft while crafting a fictional narrative that engages and entertains.

Critical Reception: Authenticity and Cinematic Appeal: The chapter delves into the critical reception of "Draft Day" with a focus on how authenticity in depicting the NFL Draft contributed to its cinematic appeal. It examines reviews that assess the film's ability to capture the essence of draft day while also acknowledging its merits as an engaging work of fiction.

The analysis considers how the film's reception reflects the delicate balance between realism and cinematic storytelling.

Legacy: Impact on Perceptions of the NFL Draft

Influence on Audience Perceptions: Shaping Draft-Day Imaginations: The chapter concludes by reflecting on the film's legacy and its impact on audience perceptions of the NFL Draft. It explores how "Draft Day" has contributed to shaping imaginations and expectations surrounding the draft process. The analysis considers the enduring resonance of the film in the minds of football enthusiasts and its place in the broader cultural conversation about the intersection of sports and cinema.

Conclusion: "Draft Day" as a Cinematic Drafting Experience

In conclusion, "Draft Day" provides a cinematic drafting experience that combines the suspenseful and strategic elements of the NFL Draft with the human stories that define the sport. The film's portrayal of the draft room dynamics, strategic maneuvering, and the personal challenges faced by players adds depth to its narrative. "Draft Day" stands as a unique entry in the sports cinema genre, offering audiences an inside look at the high-stakes world of the NFL Draft while delivering a compelling and entertaining story.

### Kevin Costner Leads Ensemble Cast

In the realm of sports cinema, "Draft Day" (2014) stands out not only for its gripping portrayal of the NFL Draft but also for its ensemble cast led by the seasoned actor Kevin Costner. This chapter explores Costner's role as the linchpin of the film, analyzing his performance, the dynamics within the ensemble cast, and the impact of his character on the overall narrative.

Introduction: Casting Kevin Costner

Costner's Legacy in Sports Films: Before delving into Costner's role in "Draft Day," this section sets the stage by examining Kevin Costner's legacy in the realm of sports films. From "Bull Durham" to "Field of Dreams," Costner has established himself as a prominent figure in sports cinema. The analysis reflects on his previous roles and the expectations that come with casting him in a sports-themed narrative.

The Choice for Sonny Weaver Jr.: The chapter then explores the casting decision that brought Kevin Costner into the role of Sonny Weaver Jr., the general manager of the Cleveland Browns. It delves into the considerations behind selecting Costner for this pivotal character and the anticipation that accompanied his portrayal of a figure navigating the high-stakes world of the NFL Draft.

Sonny Weaver Jr.: Costner's Role as the Draft-Day Architect

Character Introduction: Unpacking Sonny Weaver Jr.: This section provides an introduction to Sonny Weaver Jr., the central character portrayed by Costner. It analyzes the character's background, motivations, and the challenges he faces as the architect of the Cleveland Browns' draft day. The analysis considers how Costner brings depth to the character, balancing the pressures of his professional role with personal complexities.

Costner's Approach to Sonny Weaver Jr.: The chapter then explores Costner's approach to portraying Sonny Weaver Jr. It delves into the actor's methods, his understanding of the character, and the nuances he brings to the role. The analysis considers how Costner's portrayal contributes to the audience's connection with Sonny, making him a relatable and compelling focal point for the film's narrative.

Ensemble Dynamics: The Team Behind the Team

The Cleveland Browns' Front Office: Chemistry and Conflict: "Draft Day" introduces a diverse ensemble of characters within the Cleveland Browns' front office. This section explores the dynamics among the cast, including Jennifer Garner as Ali Parker, Denis Leary as Coach Penn, and Frank Langella as Anthony Molina. The analysis delves into the chemistry and conflicts within this team behind the team, highlighting how each actor contributes to the ensemble's overall effectiveness.

Supporting Cast: Scouts, Agents, and Players: Beyond the front office, "Draft Day" features a supporting cast of scouts, agents, and players, each playing a crucial role in the draft day narrative. This exploration considers the contributions of actors such as Chadwick Boseman, Arian Foster, and Terry Crews. The analysis reflects on how the supporting cast enriches the film's tapestry, adding depth to the various perspectives involved in the draft process.

Costner and Garner: On-Screen Chemistry

Dynamic Between Sonny Weaver Jr. and Ali Parker: A significant aspect of "Draft Day" is the on-screen chemistry between Kevin Costner and Jennifer Garner, who portrays Ali Parker, the team's salary cap manager. This section examines the dynamic between Sonny and Ali, analyzing the nuances of their professional and personal interactions. The analysis considers how Costner and Garner's performances contribute to the authenticity and emotional resonance of their on-screen relationship.

Professionalism and Personal Dynamics: Balancing Act: The chapter explores the balancing act between professionalism and personal dynamics in the relationship between Sonny and Ali. It delves into the challenges faced by characters navigating a professional setting while also dealing with personal entanglements. The analysis reflects on how Costner and Garner bring authenticity to their characters, creating a believable and engaging dynamic.

Costner's Leadership Presence: The General Manager's Dilemma

Leadership on Display: Sonny Weaver Jr.'s Dilemma: Kevin Costner's portrayal of Sonny Weaver Jr. extends beyond individual scenes to encapsulate the overarching leadership dilemma faced by the character. This section dissects how Costner embodies the challenges of being a general manager on draft day, including decision-making under pressure, negotiating trades, and managing the expectations of the team's owner and fans.

Conflict Resolution and Tough Choices: The chapter then explores Costner's depiction of Sonny's conflict resolution and the tough choices he must make. It analyzes specific scenes where the character is forced to navigate conflicting interests, showcasing Costner's ability to convey the internal struggles and external pressures faced by a general manager in the midst of draft-day decisions.

Cinematic Moments: Costner's Impactful Scenes

Key Scenes: Dramatic Peaks and Emotional Valleys: "Draft Day" is punctuated by key scenes that define the narrative and the characters' arcs. This section delves into specific moments that showcase Kevin Costner's impactful performance. From high-stakes negotiations to emotional revelations, the analysis explores how Costner elevates these scenes, contributing to the film's overall emotional resonance.

Monologues and Speeches: Costner's Art of Persuasion: Costner's performance in "Draft Day" includes notable monologues and speeches that shape the character's journey. This part of the chapter dissects these moments, analyzing Costner's art of persuasion and the impact of his delivery on the audience. The analysis considers how these monologues contribute to the film's themes and the development of Sonny Weaver Jr.'s character.

Reception: Costner's Return to Sports Cinema

Critical Acclaim: Costner's Performance in Focus: The chapter explores the critical reception of "Draft Day," with a specific focus on the acclaim for Kevin Costner's performance. It delves into reviews that highlight the actor's return to sports cinema and the effectiveness of his portrayal in anchoring the film. The analysis considers how Costner's presence contributed to the overall success of "Draft Day."

Audience Response: Costner's Enduring Appeal: Beyond critical acclaim, the chapter reflects on the audience response to Costner's performance in "Draft Day." It explores how the actor's enduring appeal, especially in sports-themed narratives, resonated with viewers. The analysis considers the impact of Costner's presence on the film's box office performance and its lasting impression on audiences.

Conclusion: Kevin Costner and the Draft-Day Legacy

In conclusion, Kevin Costner's portrayal of Sonny Weaver Jr. in "Draft Day" cements the actor's legacy in sports cinema. His leadership presence, on-screen chemistry with Jennifer Garner, and impactful performances in key scenes contribute to the film's success. Costner's return to the realm of sports-themed narratives with "Draft Day" adds another layer to his storied career, creating a lasting legacy within the intersection of sports and cinema.

## More Character Study Than Hard-Hitting Drama

In the landscape of sports cinema, "Draft Day" (2014) stands as a distinctive entry, choosing to navigate the intense world of the NFL Draft through the lens of character study rather than relying solely on the traditional tropes of hard-hitting sports drama. This chapter delves into the film's unique approach, examining how it prioritizes character development, interpersonal dynamics, and the human side of the NFL Draft over bombastic action sequences and intense gameplay.

Introduction: Redefining the Sports Drama Paradigm

Setting the Stage: Traditional vs. Character-Driven Sports Dramas: Before exploring "Draft Day," this section provides an overview of the traditional paradigm of sports dramas, emphasizing intense action sequences, on-field heroics, and the physicality of the sport. The analysis then introduces the unconventional approach of "Draft Day," focusing on character study as the driving force behind the narrative.

Breaking the Mold: Character-Driven Narratives in Sports Films: The chapter sets out to examine how "Draft Day" breaks away from the established mold of sports dramas, choosing a more intimate and character-driven narrative. It explores the risks and rewards associated with this approach, highlighting the film's commitment to presenting the NFL Draft as a deeply personal and emotionally charged experience.

Character Complexity: Sonny Weaver Jr.'s Journey

Sonny Weaver Jr.: A General Manager's Odyssey: This section embarks on an in-depth analysis of the central character, Sonny Weaver Jr., portrayed by Kevin Costner. It delves into the character's complexity, motivations, and the evolution of his journey throughout the film. The analysis explores how "Draft Day" transforms the figure of a general manager into a multi-dimensional character, inviting the audience to invest in his personal and professional struggles.

Personal and Professional Intersection: Balancing Acts: The chapter examines the delicate balance between Sonny Weaver Jr.'s personal and professional life. It dissects how the film weaves a narrative that explores the intersection of these two aspects, giving equal weight to Sonny's decisions in the draft room and the impact they have on his relationships outside the realm of football. The analysis considers the effectiveness of this approach in humanizing the character.

Interpersonal Dynamics: Relationships Behind the Scenes

Ali Parker and Sonny: Beyond Professionalism: A significant aspect of "Draft Day" is the exploration of relationships behind the scenes, particularly that between Sonny Weaver Jr. and Ali Parker, portrayed by Jennifer Garner. This section dissects how the film navigates their professional and personal dynamics, emphasizing the intricacies of workplace relationships in the high-pressure environment of the NFL Draft.

Family Ties: Sonny's Personal Sphere: Beyond the front office, the chapter explores Sonny's family dynamics, providing insight into his relationships with his mother, ex-wife, and potential fatherhood. It considers how these familial ties contribute to the character study aspect of the film, painting a more comprehensive picture of Sonny Weaver Jr. beyond his role as a general manager.

Supporting Cast: A Tapestry of Personalities

Cleveland Browns Ensemble: Individual Stories, Collective Impact: "Draft Day" boasts a rich ensemble cast beyond the central characters. This section analyzes the supporting cast, including Denis Leary as Coach Penn, Frank Langella as Anthony Molina, and Chadwick Boseman as Vontae Mack. The analysis explores how the film intricately weaves together individual stories to create a tapestry of personalities, each contributing to the overall character study.

Scouts, Players, and Agents: The Human Element of the Draft: The chapter delves into the portrayal of scouts, players, and agents, emphasizing the human element of the draft process. It explores how "Draft Day" invests time in developing these characters, highlighting their aspirations, struggles, and the impact of the draft on their lives beyond the football field. The analysis considers the film's commitment to humanizing all facets of the NFL Draft.

Dialogue-Driven Drama: Tension in Words, Not Plays

Draft Room Negotiations: Tension Beyond the Field: Unlike traditional sports dramas that rely on intense on-field action, "Draft Day" derives its tension from dialogue-driven negotiations in the draft room. This section explores how the film transforms verbal exchanges, trades, and strategic discussions into sources of dramatic intensity. The analysis considers the effectiveness of this approach in creating a unique form of sports drama that hinges on the power of words.

Monologues and Speeches: Emotional Peaks in Verbal Form: The chapter dissects specific monologues and speeches within the film, emphasizing their role as emotional peaks. It explores how these verbal expressions become pivotal moments, driving the narrative forward and providing insight into the characters' motivations and conflicts. The analysis reflects on the film's ability to elevate dialogue to the forefront of its dramatic storytelling.

Emotional Resonance: Beyond the Scoreboard

The Draft Day Emotional Quotient: "Draft Day" prioritizes emotional resonance over scoreboard victories. This section delves into the emotional quotient of the film, exploring how it connects with the audience on a personal and heartfelt level. The analysis considers the moments that evoke empathy, investment, and a range of emotions beyond the thrill of victory or the agony of defeat traditionally associated with sports dramas.

Impact Beyond the Game: Lessons and Reflections: The chapter reflects on the broader impact of "Draft Day," considering the lessons and reflections it offers beyond the realm of football. It examines how the character-driven narrative extends its influence into themes of personal growth, resilience, and the intricate nature of decision-making. The analysis considers the lasting resonance of the film's character study beyond the confines of the sports genre.

Critical Reception: Praise for Character Depth

Critical Acclaim: Appreciation for Nuanced Characterization: This section explores the critical reception of "Draft Day," focusing on the appreciation for its nuanced characterization and character study approach. The analysis delves into reviews that commend the film for prioritizing the human side of the NFL Draft, providing depth to characters, and subverting expectations within the sports drama genre.

Audience Response: Connection Through Characters: The chapter reflects on the audience response to the film's character-driven narrative. It considers how viewers connect with the characters on a personal level, transcending the boundaries of sports fandom. The analysis explores how the film's approach resonates with a broader audience, inviting them to invest in the emotional journeys of the characters.

Conclusion: "Draft Day" and the Evolution of Sports Cinema

In conclusion, "Draft Day" emerges as a trailblazer in the evolution of sports cinema, challenging the traditional narrative structures of sports dramas. By prioritizing character study over hard-hitting action, the film provides a fresh perspective on the NFL Draft, offering a more intimate and emotionally charged portrayal. As the chapter concludes, it reflects on how "Draft Day" contributes to the ongoing evolution of sports cinema, inviting audiences to experience the human side of athletic pursuits and the profound impact they have on individuals both on and off the field.

## Piggybacking on Real Draft Intrigue

Within the realm of sports cinema, "Draft Day" (2014) distinguishes itself by intertwining its narrative with the real-life intrigue and excitement of the NFL Draft. This chapter delves into how the film capitalizes on the genuine drama of the draft process, enhancing its storytelling with a backdrop of authentic football dynamics, trades, and the unpredictable nature of selecting future NFL stars.

Introduction: Merging Fiction with Reality

The NFL Draft as a Cinematic Backdrop: Before exploring how "Draft Day" piggybacks on real draft intrigue, this section sets the stage by discussing the significance of the NFL Draft as a cinematic backdrop. It explores the inherent drama and anticipation associated with the draft, detailing its impact on fans, teams, and the broader sports landscape. The analysis establishes the real-life context that "Draft Day" leverages to enrich its narrative.

The Fusion of Fact and Fiction: Creating Cinematic Tension: The chapter emphasizes the film's unique approach of merging fact and fiction, intertwining a scripted narrative with the genuine excitement and tension of the NFL Draft. It delves into how "Draft Day" strategically incorporates real elements of the draft process to enhance its cinematic tension, creating an immersive experience for both football enthusiasts and general audiences.

Authenticity in Draft-Day Dynamics

Real Draft Traditions: Grounding the Film in Reality: This section explores how "Draft Day" grounds itself in reality by incorporating authentic draft traditions. From the commissioner's announcements to the buzz surrounding top prospects, the film mirrors the actual rituals of the NFL Draft. The analysis considers how these details contribute to the film's authenticity, creating a sense of familiarity for audiences familiar with the draft process.

Scouting Reports and Player Profiles: Blurring Fictional Lines: The chapter delves into the inclusion of scouting reports, player profiles, and expert analyses within the film. It analyzes how "Draft Day" blurs the lines between fiction and reality by presenting information in a manner reminiscent of actual draft broadcasts. The analysis reflects on the film's commitment to simulating the intricacies of the scouting and selection process.

Strategic Trades: Crafting Drama Through Deals

The Art of the Trade: Reflecting Real Front Office Dynamics: "Draft Day" places a significant emphasis on strategic trades, mirroring the real dynamics of NFL front offices. This section explores how the film captures the intricacies of trade negotiations, reflecting the calculated risks and rewards that teams face during the draft. The analysis considers the film's portrayal of the chess game played by general managers to secure the best possible picks.

Incorporating Real Draft-Day Trades: Nod to Football Enthusiasts: The chapter delves into how "Draft Day" incorporates real draft-day trades into its narrative. By referencing actual transactions from NFL history, the film pays homage to football enthusiasts who follow the sport closely. The analysis considers how these nods to real-life events add an extra layer of excitement for fans, creating a sense of shared knowledge and insider appreciation.

The Unpredictability of Selections: Embracing Real Draft Surprises

Capturing the Unpredictable Nature of the Draft: This section explores how "Draft Day" embraces the unpredictable nature of the draft, a hallmark of real draft events. It analyzes how the film strategically introduces unexpected twists and turns, mirroring the surprises that often unfold during the actual selection process. The analysis considers the film's ability to capture the suspense and excitement associated with unanticipated draft-day developments.

Player Reactions and Draft-Day Drama: Realism in Performance: The chapter delves into the realistic portrayal of player reactions and draft-day drama within the film. It explores how "Draft Day" captures the emotional highs and lows experienced by players as they wait to hear their names called. The analysis reflects on the authenticity of the performances, considering how the film effectively conveys the impact of the draft on the lives of the athletes.

Media Presence and Fan Engagement

Media Coverage: Reflecting the Spotlight on Draft Day: This section examines how "Draft Day" integrates media coverage, reflecting the intense spotlight that accompanies the NFL Draft. The film captures the energy of draft-day broadcasts, press conferences, and the media frenzy surrounding top prospects. The analysis considers how these elements contribute to the film's immersion in the real-world atmosphere of draft day.

Fan Engagement: Tapping into the Passion of Football Fandom: The chapter explores how "Draft Day" taps into the passion of football fandom by depicting the reactions of fans throughout the film. It analyzes how the narrative incorporates the emotional investment of supporters, reflecting the genuine enthusiasm and dedication of football aficionados during the draft. The analysis considers the film's ability to resonate with a diverse audience, from die-hard fans to casual viewers.

Navigating Real-Life Challenges: Timeliness and Relevance

Timeliness of Release: Aligning with Draft Season Excitement: This section explores the timeliness of "Draft Day's" release, aligning with the heightened excitement and anticipation surrounding the NFL Draft season. The analysis reflects on how the film strategically positions itself to leverage the real-time enthusiasm generated by draft-related discussions and events. It considers the impact of releasing the film during a period of heightened football fervor.

Relevance Beyond the Draft Season: Prolonged Impact and Discussions: The chapter delves into how "Draft Day" maintains its relevance beyond the immediate draft season. It analyzes the film's ability to spark prolonged discussions and engage audiences throughout the year. The analysis considers how the film's narrative, anchored in the authentic dynamics of the NFL Draft, sustains its impact, prompting ongoing conversations among fans and film enthusiasts alike.

Critical Reception: Acknowledging the Fusion of Real and Reel

Critical Acclaim: Recognition of Realism and Football Authenticity: This section explores the critical reception of "Draft Day," with a focus on the recognition of its realism and football authenticity. The analysis delves into reviews that acknowledge the film's ability to seamlessly blend real and reel elements, creating a cinematic experience that resonates with both football enthusiasts and a broader audience. It considers how the film's unique approach garnered praise for its authenticity.

Audience Response: Engaging Football Fans and Beyond: The chapter reflects on the audience response to "Draft Day," particularly the engagement of football fans and a wider demographic. It considers how the film's fusion of real draft intrigue with cinematic storytelling appealed to viewers on multiple levels. The analysis explores the film's success in reaching both dedicated football enthusiasts and those less familiar with the intricacies of the draft.

Conclusion: "Draft Day" and the Legacy of Realism in Sports Cinema

In conclusion, "Draft Day" leaves an indelible mark on sports cinema by effectively piggybacking on real draft intrigue. By weaving authentic elements of the NFL Draft into its narrative fabric, the film creates a compelling and immersive experience for audiences. As the chapter concludes, it reflects on how "Draft Day" contributes to the legacy of realism in sports cinema, inviting viewers to embrace the genuine excitement, drama, and unpredictability that define the world of professional football.

## Chapter 11: Themes and Comparisons Across the Films
### Shifting Portrayals of Race Relations

The cinematic landscape of NFL films serves as a mirror to the broader societal shifts in attitudes and perceptions of race relations. As we delve into the thematic exploration of these films, one of the significant threads woven into the narrative tapestry is the evolving portrayal of race relations. This chapter critically examines how these NFL films tackle the complexities of race, from the early depictions in the 1970s to the nuanced narratives of more recent productions.

Introduction: Race as a Central Theme in NFL Films

Setting the Stage: Historical Context and Cinematic Representations: Before delving into the specific films, the introduction contextualizes the historical backdrop against which these films were produced. It explores the broader sociocultural climate and the changing landscape of race relations in the United States. The analysis considers how NFL films, as both products and shapers of culture, contribute to the ongoing conversation about race.

Evolution of Representations: A Journey Through Decades: The chapter introduces the central theme of the shifting portrayals of race relations in NFL films. It emphasizes that these cinematic representations are not static but have evolved over the decades, reflecting the changing perspectives and attitudes towards race in society. The analysis sets the stage for a nuanced exploration of how each film contributes to this evolving narrative.

1970s: Breaking Ground and Pioneering Narratives

The Longest Yard (1974): Rebellion and Racial Solidarity: This section examines how "The Longest Yard" (1974) tackles issues of race within the context of a prison football team. It delves into the film's portrayal of rebellion, racial solidarity, and the challenges faced by African American characters. The analysis considers how the film, set against a backdrop of incarceration, contributes to the 1970s discourse on race and activism.

North Dallas Forty (1979): Early Critiques of Exploitation: The chapter moves on to "North Dallas Forty" (1979) and its exploration of race within the professional football arena. It analyzes the film's early critiques of exploitation, shedding light on the challenges faced by African American players. The analysis considers how the film contributes to the discourse on racial dynamics within the sports industry during this era.

1980s-1990s: Navigating Stereotypes and Expanding Narratives

Brian's Song (1971) and Its Long-Lasting Impact: Before delving into the 1980s and 1990s films, this section reflects on the lasting impact of "Brian's Song" (1971) in shaping the portrayal of race relations. It considers the groundbreaking nature of the film and its depiction of an unlikely friendship that defied racial stereotypes, laying the groundwork for more complex narratives in subsequent decades.

The Replacements (2000): Comedy, Race, and Unity: Moving into the 2000s, this part of the chapter explores how "The Replacements" (2000) approaches race within the context of a comedic sports film. It analyzes the film's portrayal of unity among replacement players and how it navigates racial dynamics in a lighthearted manner. The analysis considers the role of humor in addressing race-related themes within the sports comedy genre.

Any Given Sunday (1999): Race, Power, and Institutional Critique: The focus then shifts to "Any Given Sunday" (1999) and its portrayal of race, power, and institutional critique within the hyperkinetic world of professional football. The analysis delves into how the film explores racial tensions among players, coaches, and team owners, offering a multifaceted examination of race relations within the NFL.

2000s-2010s: From Uplifting Narratives to Nuanced Realism

The Blind Side (2009): Feel-Good Narratives and Racial Dynamics: This section explores "The Blind Side" (2009) and its feel-good narrative that intersects with racial dynamics. The analysis delves into the film's portrayal of the white savior trope and the underlying racial and economic issues simmering beneath the uplifting tale. It considers how the film navigates these complexities within the framework of a heartwarming true story.

Invincible (2006): Vince Papale's Journey and Unity: Moving to "Invincible" (2006), the chapter analyzes the film's depiction of Vince Papale's improbable journey to the NFL and its portrayal of unity within a racially diverse team. The analysis considers how the film uses a real-life underdog story to address themes of race and camaraderie, reflecting the changing dynamics within sports narratives.

1990s-2000s: Jerry Maguire and the Modern Athlete's Dilemma

Jerry Maguire (1996): Show Me the Money and Racial Dynamics: This section explores "Jerry Maguire" (1996) and its iconic catchphrase "Show me the money." The analysis delves into the origins of this modern catchphrase and its implications for racial dynamics within the sports industry. It considers how the film navigates the complexities of race and economic empowerment in the context of athlete representation.

2010s-2020s: Modern Narratives and Broader Perspectives

Draft Day (2014): Real Draft Intrigue and Diverse Perspectives: Before concluding the chapter, this section reflects on "Draft Day" (2014) and its integration of real draft intrigue within the broader narrative. The analysis considers how the film reflects diverse perspectives on race, both within the front office and among the players. It explores how the film contributes to the evolving conversation about race relations in the NFL.

Conclusion: A Tapestry of Perspectives and Ongoing Dialogue

In conclusion, this chapter reflects on the evolving tapestry of perspectives on race relations within NFL films. It acknowledges the strides made in portraying diverse narratives, from breaking ground in the 1970s to navigating stereotypes in the 1980s and 1990s, and embracing nuanced realism in the

2000s and beyond. The analysis emphasizes the ongoing dialogue initiated by these films, acknowledging their role in shaping and reflecting the broader societal conversations about race in America.

## Football as an Allegory for Life's Lessons

The intersection of football and cinema provides a unique canvas for filmmakers to explore profound themes that extend beyond the gridiron. This chapter delves into the captivating motif of football as an allegory for life's lessons across a spectrum of NFL films. From triumphs and defeats to teamwork and individual resilience, these movies weave a narrative tapestry that transcends the boundaries of the sport, offering poignant reflections on the human experience.

Introduction: Beyond the Game - Football as a Metaphor

The Symbolism of the Gridiron: Before delving into specific films, the introduction establishes the symbolic significance of the football field as a microcosm of life. It explores the inherent drama, competition, and camaraderie that make football a potent metaphor for the human experience. The analysis sets the stage for an exploration of how NFL films leverage this metaphor to convey universal truths and life's lessons.

The Cinematic Power of Allegory: The chapter emphasizes the cinematic power of allegory, showcasing how filmmakers harness the visual and emotional impact of football to convey broader themes. It considers the unique ability of the sport to serve as a canvas for storytelling, allowing filmmakers to draw parallels between the challenges faced on the field and the complexities of life off the field.

1970s-1980s: Lessons in Rebellion, Individuality, and Team Dynamics

The Longest Yard (1974): Rebellion and the Pursuit of Redemption: This section explores how "The Longest Yard" (1974) uses football as an allegory for rebellion and the pursuit of redemption. The analysis delves into the film's portrayal of individuality within a team setting, drawing parallels between the characters' personal struggles and the challenges faced on the football field. It considers how the game becomes a metaphor for overcoming societal barriers.

North Dallas Forty (1979): Individuality Amidst Institutional Pressures: Moving to "North Dallas Forty" (1979), the chapter examines how the film navigates the theme of individuality amidst institutional pressures. It analyzes the protagonist's journey as an allegory for self-discovery and resilience, emphasizing how football serves as a backdrop for exploring the tension between personal identity and conformity within the context of professional sports.

1990s: Lessons in Perseverance, Sacrifice, and Redemption

Rudy (1993): The Ultimate Underdog's Journey: This part of the chapter focuses on "Rudy" (1993) and its portrayal of football as a metaphor for perseverance and the pursuit of one's dreams. The analysis delves into Rudy Ruettiger's underdog journey, exploring how the sport becomes a vehicle for personal growth and redemption. It considers the film's enduring appeal as a testament to the universal themes embedded in the game.

Any Given Sunday (1999): Life's Brutal Realities and Team Dynamics: Shifting to "Any Given Sunday" (1999), the chapter explores how the film tackles life's brutal realities through the lens of professional football. It analyzes the allegorical use of the sport to convey the harsh lessons of success and failure, emphasizing the complex team dynamics as a microcosm of broader societal struggles. The analysis considers how football becomes a canvas for exploring the human condition.

2000s: Lessons in Unity, Mentorship, and Overcoming Odds

The Replacements (2000): Ragtag Unity and Overcoming Differences: This section delves into "The Replacements" (2000) and its use of football as an allegory for unity and overcoming differences. The analysis explores how the ragtag team of replacement players becomes a symbol of diverse individuals coming together for a common goal. It considers the film's portrayal of teamwork as a universal lesson applicable beyond the football field.

Invincible (2006): Vince Papale's Journey as a Blueprint for Overcoming Odds: Moving to "Invincible" (2006), the chapter examines the film's portrayal of football as a blueprint for overcoming odds. It analyzes Vince Papale's journey from unlikely tryout to NFL player as an allegory for resilience and the pursuit of personal excellence. The analysis considers how the film's underdog narrative resonates with audiences as a source of inspiration.

2010s-2020s: Lessons in Mentorship, Identity, and Team Bonding

The Blind Side (2009): Mentorship, Identity, and Transformative Relationships: This part of the chapter focuses on "The Blind Side" (2009) and its use of football as an allegory for mentorship, personal identity, and transformative relationships. The analysis explores how the sport becomes a backdrop for exploring the profound impact of nurturing connections and the transformative power of compassion. It considers the film's allegorical exploration of the complexities of human relationships.

Draft Day (2014): Front Office Strategies as Metaphors for Life's Decisions: Shifting to "Draft Day" (2014), the chapter explores how the film leverages the NFL Draft as an allegory for life's decisions. It analyzes the strategic choices made by front office executives as metaphors for the broader decisions individuals face in their personal and professional lives. The analysis considers how the film's exploration of decision-making resonates with audiences on a universal level.

Conclusion: The Enduring Power of Football as Allegory

In conclusion, the chapter reflects on the enduring power of football as an allegory for life's lessons within NFL films. It acknowledges the diverse ways in which filmmakers have harnessed the sport's symbolism to convey universal truths, from individual resilience and team dynamics to the pursuit of dreams and overcoming societal barriers. The analysis emphasizes the lasting impact of these allegorical narratives, underscoring the timeless and universal themes embedded in the game of football.

## Critiques of Commercialization and Culture

In the realm where the gridiron meets the silver screen, NFL films serve as a lens through which filmmakers explore the intricate relationship between football, commercialization, and culture. This chapter delves into the thought-provoking theme of critiques of commercialization and culture within the context of iconic NFL movies. From examining the impact of corporate interests on the purity of the game to probing the cultural dynamics reflected in football narratives, these films offer a nuanced exploration of the intersection between sport and society.

Introduction: The Business of the Game

Football as Big Business: Before delving into specific films, the introduction sets the stage by addressing the evolving landscape of professional football as big business. It explores how the sport, once rooted in local communities, transformed into a multibillion-dollar industry, attracting corporate interests that shaped the game's trajectory. The analysis highlights the duality of football as both a cultural phenomenon and a commercial enterprise, providing the backdrop for the exploration of critiques within the films.

The Cinematic Mirror: Reflecting Commercial Realities: The chapter emphasizes the unique role of cinema in reflecting and critiquing the commercial realities of professional football. It introduces the idea that NFL films, as a form of cultural expression, have the power to act as a cinematic mirror, reflecting the commercialization of the sport and offering commentary on its implications for the culture at large.

1970s-1980s: Dawn of Commercial Pressures

The Longest Yard (1974): Football Behind Bars and Commercial Interests: This section explores how "The Longest Yard" (1974) provides an early glimpse into the impact of commercial interests on the game, even within the unconventional setting of a prison. The analysis delves into the portrayal of corporate pressures and the clash between the purity of the sport and the influence of outside forces, setting the stage for subsequent critiques in later decades.

North Dallas Forty (1979): Corporate Control in Professional Football: Moving to "North Dallas Forty" (1979), the chapter examines how the film critiques corporate control within professional football. It analyzes the narrative's exploration of the tensions between players and management, shedding light on the commercialization of the sport and its impact on the athletes' autonomy. The analysis considers how the film lays the foundation for later examinations of corporate influence.

1990s: The Spectacle of Entertainment and Corporate Intrusion

Any Given Sunday (1999): The Spectacle of Entertainment and Its Costs: This part of the chapter focuses on "Any Given Sunday" (1999) and its critique of the spectacle of entertainment within professional football. The analysis explores how the film portrays the commercial pressures to turn the sport into a grand spectacle, emphasizing the costs, both physical and cultural, associated with the pursuit of entertainment value. It considers how the film anticipates the evolving dynamics of football as mass entertainment.

Jerry Maguire (1996): Show Me the Money and Its Cultural Ramifications: Shifting to "Jerry Maguire" (1996), the chapter examines how the film delves into the cultural ramifications of the sport's commercialization. It analyzes the iconic catchphrase "Show me the money" as a symbol of the commodification of athletes and the impact of corporate interests on player-agent relationships. The analysis considers how the film contributes to the broader conversation about the business side of professional football.

2000s-2010s: Balancing Act and the Price of Success

The Blind Side (2009): Commercialization, Success, and the American Dream: This section explores "The Blind Side" (2009) and its nuanced portrayal of the intersection between commercialization, success, and the American Dream within the context of professional football. The analysis delves into how the film navigates the challenges of balancing commercial interests with the pursuit of success, particularly for athletes coming from disadvantaged backgrounds. It considers how the film critiques societal expectations and the commodification of talent.

Draft Day (2014): Front Office Strategies and Corporate Intrusion: Moving to "Draft Day" (2014), the chapter analyzes how the film explores the intricacies of front office strategies and the corporate intrusion into the decision-making processes of professional football. It delves into the high-stakes world of the NFL Draft as a microcosm of corporate influence, considering how the film critiques the commodification of talent and the impact of corporate interests on team dynamics.

Conclusion: Navigating the Crossroads of Culture and Commerce

In conclusion, this chapter reflects on the intricate dance between culture and commerce within NFL films. It acknowledges the films' capacity to act as a critical mirror, offering insights into the evolving dynamics of professional football as it grapples with the pressures of commercialization. The analysis emphasizes the enduring relevance of these critiques, highlighting the ongoing dialogue within the films about the delicate balance between preserving the essence of the game and succumbing to the demands of corporate interests.

## New Styles and Perspectives in Sports Films

Within the tapestry of NFL films, the narrative canvas has evolved, showcasing not only the sport of football but also the evolving styles and perspectives in sports filmmaking. This chapter explores the innovative storytelling techniques, cinematographic choices, and thematic perspectives that distinguish a new era of sports films, with a focus on those centered around the NFL. From the experimental approaches of the 1990s to the contemporary era's embrace of diverse voices, these films contribute to a dynamic landscape that transcends traditional sports storytelling.

Introduction: The Evolution of Sports Filmmaking

The Shifting Landscape of Sports Cinema: Before delving into specific films, the introduction sets the stage by addressing the broader evolution of sports cinema. It explores the transformation from conventional sports narratives to more nuanced and experimental approaches, highlighting the changing tastes of audiences and the influence of contemporary storytelling trends. The analysis underscores the importance of NFL films in reflecting and contributing to this evolving cinematic landscape.

Breaking Away from Conventions: The chapter emphasizes the significance of NFL films in breaking away from conventional sports storytelling. It introduces the idea that these films, rather than adhering to formulaic approaches, have embraced new styles and perspectives, offering audiences a fresh and diverse range of narratives within the realm of football.

1990s: Experimentation and Unconventional Narratives

Any Given Sunday (1999): Oliver Stone's Cinematic Boldness: This section explores how "Any Given Sunday" (1999) embodies the experimentation and cinematic boldness of the 1990s. The analysis delves into Oliver Stone's hyperkinetic approach, examining the film's unconventional narrative structure, visual flourishes, and thematic complexity. It considers how "Any Given Sunday" set a precedent for a more daring and stylistically diverse era of sports filmmaking.

Jerry Maguire (1996): The Birth of the Modern Sports Dramedy: Moving to "Jerry Maguire" (1996), the chapter examines the film's contribution to the birth of the modern sports dramedy. It analyzes how the film seamlessly blends elements of drama and comedy, challenging traditional genre boundaries. The analysis considers the impact of "Jerry Maguire" in shaping the expectations of audiences and filmmakers regarding the potential for nuanced storytelling within sports narratives.

2000s-2010s: Diversity of Voices and Storytelling Approaches

The Blind Side (2009): Blending Social Issues with Sports Drama: This part of the chapter focuses on "The Blind Side" (2009) and its approach to blending social issues with sports drama. The analysis explores how the film navigates themes of race, socioeconomic disparities, and cultural dynamics, enriching the traditional sports narrative with layers of societal commentary. It considers the film's role in expanding the scope of storytelling within the genre.

Draft Day (2014): A Character Study in the Heart of Football Operations: Shifting to "Draft Day" (2014), the chapter analyzes how the film represents a character study embedded in the heart of football operations. It explores the film's unique storytelling perspective, delving into the intricate world of front office strategies and decision-making processes. The analysis considers how "Draft Day" contributes to a more cerebral and strategic subgenre within sports filmmaking.

2010s-2020s: Inclusivity and Representation

Brian's Song (1971) Revisited: Pioneering Inclusivity in Football Narratives: This section revisits "Brian's Song" (1971) to highlight its pioneering role in inclusivity within football narratives. The analysis explores the film's groundbreaking portrayal of the friendship between Brian Piccolo and Gale Sayers, emphasizing its significance in presenting diverse perspectives and challenging prevailing norms. It considers how "Brian's Song" laid the groundwork for more inclusive storytelling in contemporary NFL films.

Silver Screen Legends: Embracing Diverse Voices and Narratives: The chapter concludes by reflecting on the broader landscape of NFL films in the current era. It acknowledges the industry's efforts to embrace diverse voices and narratives, showcasing stories that resonate with a wide range of audiences. The analysis emphasizes the importance of continued inclusivity and representation in shaping the future of sports filmmaking.

Conclusion: The Ever-Expanding Palette of NFL Films

In conclusion, the chapter reflects on the ever-expanding palette of NFL films, highlighting the industry's journey from conventional narratives to the embrace of diverse styles and perspectives. It acknowledges the influence of key films in shaping the evolving landscape of sports filmmaking, providing audiences with an array of storytelling experiences within the realm of football. The analysis underscores the importance of ongoing innovation, inclusivity, and representation in ensuring the continued vitality of NFL films in the years to come.

## Chapter 12: NFL Films' Impact on Wider Culture Catchphrases, Memorable Characters, and Moments

NFL Films, with its unique blend of cinematic storytelling and sports drama, has etched itself into the cultural fabric of football enthusiasts worldwide. Beyond the touchdowns and tackles, this chapter explores the lasting impact of NFL Films on wider culture, delving into the creation of iconic catchphrases, the development of memorable characters, and the crystallization of unforgettable moments that resonate far beyond the field.

Introduction: The Cultural Tapestry of NFL Films

The Power of Cinematic Storytelling: Before delving into specific elements, the introduction sets the stage by emphasizing the power of cinematic storytelling within NFL Films. It explores how the marriage of visual artistry and narrative innovation has elevated football from a mere sport to a cultural phenomenon. The analysis underscores the unique role of NFL Films in shaping the way audiences experience and engage with the game.

Beyond the Game: Cultural Impact and Legacy: The chapter introduces the idea that NFL Films' influence extends far beyond the game itself. It explores the cultural impact and enduring legacy of the films, emphasizing their ability to transcend the boundaries of sport and become ingrained in the collective consciousness of fans.

The Birth of Catchphrases: Immortalizing the Verbal Landscape

"The Autumn Wind is a Pirate": This section delves into the creation and impact of memorable catchphrases, starting with the iconic "The Autumn Wind is a Pirate." The analysis explores the origins of this poetic description of the Oakland Raiders, its resonance with fans, and its enduring place in football lore. It considers how catchphrases like these contribute to the rich verbal landscape of the sport.

"America's Team": Moving to the coined term "America's Team" associated with the Dallas Cowboys, the chapter examines how this catchphrase transcended its origin to become a cultural touchstone. The analysis explores the marketing genius behind the label, its influence on the Cowboys' identity, and its lasting impact on the broader perception of the team and the sport.

Memorable Characters: From Players to Narrators

John Facenda: The Voice of God: This part of the chapter focuses on John Facenda, the legendary voice behind many NFL Films productions. The analysis delves into Facenda's distinctive narration style, often referred to as "The Voice of God," and its role in shaping the emotional resonance of the films. It considers how Facenda became a cultural icon, forever linked with the evocative storytelling of NFL Films.

Steve Sabol: A Visionary Filmmaker: Shifting to Steve Sabol, the creative force behind NFL Films, the chapter explores Sabol's impact as a visionary filmmaker. The analysis examines his role in shaping the visual language of football storytelling, the development of signature techniques, and the influence of his cinematic sensibilities on the broader landscape of sports documentaries.

Unforgettable Moments: Cinematic Time Capsules

The Immaculate Reception: This section delves into specific moments captured by NFL Films, starting with the "Immaculate Reception." The analysis explores how the film immortalized this iconic play, its cultural significance in NFL history, and its enduring status as a cinematic time capsule that transports audiences back to a pivotal moment in the sport.

The Catch: Moving to "The Catch" involving Joe Montana and Dwight Clark, the chapter examines how NFL Films captured the essence of this unforgettable moment. The analysis explores the emotional weight of the play, its impact on the narrative of the game, and its enduring legacy as a symbol of athletic excellence.

Conclusion: The Enduring Legacy of NFL Films

In conclusion, the chapter reflects on the enduring legacy of NFL Films through the lens of catchphrases, memorable characters, and moments. It acknowledges the profound impact of these elements on wider culture, emphasizing how they have contributed to the cultural identity of football. The analysis underscores the role of NFL Films in not only documenting the game but also in shaping the narrative and emotional connection that fans have with the sport.

## Reinforcing and Challenging Stereotypes

NFL Films, as a cultural touchstone, holds the power not only to celebrate the triumphs and heroics of the game but also to shape and reflect societal attitudes. This chapter delves into the nuanced role of NFL Films in reinforcing and challenging stereotypes. From perpetuating traditional narratives to subverting expectations, these films navigate the complex terrain of cultural representation within the broader context of football.

Introduction: The Dual Role of Representation

The Lens of NFL Films: Before delving into specific examples, the introduction sets the stage by acknowledging the powerful role of NFL Films as a cultural lens. It explores how these films, through their portrayal of players, coaches, and narratives, influence and reflect societal perceptions. The analysis underscores the dual role of representation – both as a tool for reinforcing existing stereotypes and as a medium for challenging and reshaping them.

Football and Societal Narratives: The chapter introduces the idea that football, as depicted in NFL Films, serves as a microcosm of societal narratives. It explores how the films navigate the intricacies of race, gender, and identity, contributing to the broader conversation about representation in popular culture.

Perpetuating Stereotypes: The Familiar Narratives

The Gladiators on the Gridiron: This section explores the portrayal of football players as modern-day gladiators. The analysis delves into the cinematic language used to depict athletes as warriors on the gridiron, emphasizing physical prowess and toughness. It considers how this narrative, while iconic, may perpetuate stereotypes about masculinity and reinforce traditional expectations placed on athletes.

The Quarterback Archetype: Moving to the archetype of the quarterback, the chapter examines how NFL Films has contributed to the construction of a specific image for this position. The analysis explores the perpetuation of stereotypes related to leadership, intelligence, and race within the portrayal of quarterbacks, considering how these narratives influence societal perceptions beyond the football field.

Challenging Stereotypes: Expanding the Narrative

Breaking Racial Stereotypes: This part of the chapter focuses on instances where NFL Films challenges racial stereotypes. The analysis explores narratives that break away from traditional expectations, showcasing the intellectual prowess, leadership, and diverse experiences of players of color. It considers how these counter-narratives contribute to a more inclusive and nuanced understanding of race within the context of football.

Women in Football: Shifting to the representation of women, the chapter examines how NFL Films has navigated the evolving role of women in football. The analysis explores narratives that challenge gender stereotypes, depicting women as knowledgeable and passionate contributors to the sport. It considers how these representations contribute to the broader conversation about inclusivity and gender equality in football culture.

The Intersection of Football and Identity: Beyond Stereotypes

Identity Beyond the Field: This section delves into how NFL Films explores the multifaceted identities of players beyond their roles on the field. The analysis considers narratives that delve into personal struggles, cultural backgrounds, and community engagement, highlighting the complexity of identity within the broader context of football culture. It explores how these nuanced portrayals contribute to a more comprehensive understanding of athletes as individuals.

The Changing Face of Fandom: Moving to the representation of fans, the chapter examines how NFL Films has contributed to changing narratives around fandom. The analysis explores diverse fan experiences, challenging stereotypes about who belongs in the football community. It considers how these representations reflect and contribute to the evolving demographic landscape of football enthusiasts.

Conclusion: The Ongoing Dialogue of Representation

In conclusion, the chapter reflects on the dynamic interplay between NFL Films and societal perceptions. It acknowledges the dual role of representation – both as a perpetuator of stereotypes and a catalyst for change. The analysis emphasizes the ongoing dialogue within NFL Films, recognizing the industry's responsibility to shape narratives that reflect the diversity and complexity of the football community.

### Tangible Influences on Generations of Fans

NFL Films stands as a cultural force that transcends the boundaries of sport, leaving an indelible mark on the hearts and minds of football enthusiasts across generations. This chapter explores the tangible influences wielded by NFL Films on fans, delving into the emotional connection, community-building, and broader cultural impact that has shaped the way individuals experience and engage with the game.

Introduction: The Emotional Resonance of NFL Films

The Emotional Tapestry: Before examining specific influences, the introduction establishes the emotional resonance of NFL Films. It explores how the marriage of visual storytelling and aural artistry has created a unique emotional tapestry, weaving together the triumphs, defeats, and human stories that resonate deeply with fans. The analysis underscores the emotional connection as a driving force behind the tangible influences of NFL Films on generations of football enthusiasts.

Beyond the Highlights: Cultural Impact and Legacy: The chapter introduces the idea that the impact of NFL Films extends beyond the mere documentation of games. It explores the broader cultural impact and enduring legacy of the films, emphasizing their role in shaping the cultural identity of football and the communities of fans it has fostered.

Building a Football Community: The Shared Experience

Sunday Rituals: This section explores how NFL Films has contributed to the establishment of Sunday rituals for football fans. The analysis delves into the tradition of gathering with friends and family to watch games, examining how NFL

Films' storytelling has become an integral part of these communal experiences. It considers the role of the films in shaping the collective memory of football Sundays for fans across the globe.

Multi-Generational Fandom: Moving to the concept of multi-generational fandom, the chapter examines how NFL Films has facilitated the passing down of the love for football from one generation to the next. The analysis explores narratives that resonate across age groups, creating shared experiences that bridge generational gaps. It considers how the films have become a conduit for familial bonds centered around the game.

Cultural Artifacts: NFL Films Memorabilia and Merchandise

The Evolution of NFL Films Merchandise: This part of the chapter focuses on the creation and evolution of NFL Films merchandise. The analysis explores how the films have transcended the screen to become cultural artifacts, with fans proudly displaying memorabilia that reflects their allegiance to both the teams and the cinematic storytelling. It considers the impact of merchandise in solidifying the identity of fans within the broader football community.

Collectibles and Nostalgia: Shifting to the realm of collectibles, the chapter examines the nostalgia-driven market for vintage NFL Films memorabilia. The analysis explores how items such as old highlight reels, posters, and production artifacts have become cherished collectibles, embodying the timeless allure of football nostalgia. It considers the role of these artifacts in connecting fans across different eras.

The Power of Narratives: Shaping Fan Allegiances

Legendary Narratives and Team Allegiances: This section delves into the power of narratives in shaping fan allegiances. The analysis explores how NFL Films has contributed to the creation of legendary narratives around teams, players, and moments, influencing the emotional attachment fans develop for specific franchises. It considers the enduring impact of these narratives in cultivating a sense of belonging within the broader football community.

The Underdog Effect: Moving to the concept of the underdog effect, the chapter examines how NFL Films' storytelling has elevated certain teams or players to iconic status, especially when overcoming adversity. The analysis explores how narratives centered around underdog stories resonate deeply with fans, inspiring loyalty and passion that transcends on-field performance.

Educational Impact: From Strategy to History

Football as an Educational Tool: This part of the chapter focuses on the educational impact of NFL Films. The analysis explores how the films have served as an educational tool, providing fans with insights into the intricacies of the game. It considers the role of NFL Films in demystifying football strategy and enhancing fans' understanding of the sport, contributing to a more informed and engaged fanbase.

Preserving Football History: Shifting to the preservation of football history, the chapter examines how NFL Films has become a custodian of the game's rich heritage. The analysis explores how the films archive and present historical moments, players, and teams, contributing to the collective memory of football. It considers the role of NFL Films in ensuring that the legacy of the sport is passed down to future generations of fans.

Conclusion: The Enduring Legacy of NFL Films' Influence

In conclusion, the chapter reflects on the enduring legacy of NFL Films' tangible influences on generations of fans. It acknowledges the multifaceted impact of the films – from fostering community and shaping fan identities to serving as cultural artifacts and educational resources. The analysis emphasizes the ongoing and dynamic relationship between NFL Films and its audience, recognizing the profound and lasting imprint it has left on the collective experience of football enthusiasts.

## Conclusion
## The Definitive 10 - Ranking the Most Important NFL Films

In the grand tapestry of NFL Films' cinematic legacy, the task of distilling the most important films becomes a subjective yet essential endeavor. This concluding chapter takes on the challenge of crafting a definitive list, ranking the films that have not only shaped the narrative of football but have also left an indelible mark on the cultural landscape. The analysis considers a myriad of factors, from storytelling prowess to societal impact, aiming to provide a comprehensive overview of the films that stand as the bedrock of NFL cinematic history.

Setting the Criteria: Defining Importance

Artistic Merit and Storytelling Mastery: Before delving into the rankings, the introduction sets the criteria for defining importance. It emphasizes the artistic merit of the films, considering the mastery of storytelling techniques that have elevated certain productions to iconic status. The analysis acknowledges the role of creativity, innovation, and cinematic excellence as key factors in determining the importance of a film within the context of NFL Films.

Cultural and Societal Impact: Moving beyond the technical aspects, the chapter introduces the importance of cultural and societal impact. It explores how certain films have transcended the realm of sports, influencing societal perceptions, sparking conversations, and contributing to the broader cultural narrative. The analysis considers the lasting legacy of films that have left an indelible mark on the way football is perceived and celebrated in popular culture.

The Definitive 10: A Cinematic Countdown

10. "The Autumn Wind" (1974): The analysis begins with the cinematic poem "The Autumn Wind," exploring its significance as a cultural touchstone for the Oakland Raiders. It considers the impact of its poetic narration and distinctive imagery, examining how the film has become emblematic not only of a team but of the rugged and enigmatic spirit of football itself.

9. "America's Game" Series (2006–Present): Moving to the "America's Game" series, the chapter explores the importance of this ongoing documentary series that chronicles the stories behind each Super Bowl-winning team. The analysis delves into how the series has become a treasure trove of football history, providing in-depth narratives that humanize the players and coaches who have reached the pinnacle of the sport.

8. "The Ice Bowl" (1967): Shifting to a historic moment in football, the chapter examines "The Ice Bowl." The analysis explores how this film captures the intensity and drama of the iconic 1967 NFL Championship Game between the Green Bay Packers and the Dallas Cowboys in sub-zero temperatures. It considers the lasting impact of this film as a testament to the resilience and determination inherent in the sport.

7. "NFL Films Presents" (1967–Present): Addressing the longevity of NFL Films' impact, the analysis turns to the ongoing series "NFL Films Presents." It explores the

significance of this platform in showcasing diverse and compelling stories from the world of football. The chapter considers how this series has contributed to the democratization of football narratives, bringing a wide array of stories to audiences beyond the traditional scope of the sport.

6. "Hard Knocks" Series (2001–Present): The chapter moves to the intersection of entertainment and reality with the "Hard Knocks" series. The analysis explores the importance of this documentary-style show that takes viewers behind the scenes of NFL training camps. It considers how "Hard Knocks" has humanized players, coaches, and teams, offering an intimate look at the challenges and triumphs that unfold in the pursuit of football excellence.

5. "NFL Films Game of the Week" (1965–1981): Delving into the historical archives, the chapter explores the "NFL Films Game of the Week" series. The analysis examines how these broadcasts, narrated by John Facenda, became a pioneering effort to capture and present entire NFL games in a cinematic and storytelling format. It considers the significance of this series in laying the foundation for the distinctive cinematic language of NFL Films.

4. "A Football Life" Series (2011–Present): Turning to the personal narratives of players, coaches, and football luminaries, the chapter considers the impact of the "A Football Life" series. The analysis explores how this documentary series has humanized the legends of the game, offering a comprehensive and introspective look at the lives and careers of those who have shaped the sport.

3. "NFL Films Presents: They Call It Pro Football" (1967): Returning to a seminal moment in the history of NFL Films, the chapter examines "They Call It Pro Football." The analysis explores how this film, created by Ed Sabol and Steve Sabol, laid the foundation for the cinematic storytelling approach that would become the hallmark of NFL Films. It considers the pioneering techniques employed in this early production and its enduring influence on the art of sports documentaries.

2. "NFL Films Presents: The Power and the Glory" (1968): Moving to another landmark production, the chapter explores "The Power and the Glory." The analysis delves into how this film, which chronicled the 1968 NFL season, elevated the art of sports filmmaking. It considers the innovative narrative structure, visual storytelling techniques, and the evocative use of music that set new standards for capturing the drama and spectacle of football.

1. "NFL Films Presents: Men Who Played the Game" (1963): In the top spot of the definitive ranking, the chapter explores "Men Who Played the Game," a groundbreaking film from the early years of NFL Films. The analysis considers the importance of this production in establishing the signature style and ethos of NFL Films. It examines how "Men Who Played the Game" set the stage for a cinematic revolution in sports storytelling, creating a template that would shape the future of football documentaries.

Conclusion: The Legacy of NFL Films

In concluding the ranking, the analysis reflects on the collective legacy of these ten films. It considers how each production, in its own way, has contributed to the rich tapestry of NFL Films' storytelling, leaving an indelible mark on the cinematic history of football. The chapter underscores the enduring influence of these films, emphasizing their role in shaping not only the narrative of the game but the cultural perception of football itself. As the screen fades to black, the legacy of NFL Films continues to flicker in the hearts of fans, a testament to the artistry and impact of cinematic storytelling on the gridiron.

## Lingering Questions and Avenues for Future Study

As we bring the curtain down on the cinematic journey through the NFL, it's essential to acknowledge that the exploration of football on the silver screen is an ever-evolving narrative. This conclusion takes a reflective stance, pondering lingering questions and illuminating potential avenues for future study in the intersection of football and cinema.

Unexplored Narratives:

The landscape of football is vast and varied, and as we assess the films covered in this book, it becomes apparent that certain narratives remain untouched. The conclusion delves into the unexplored stories, personalities, and historical moments that could form the basis for future cinematic endeavors. Whether it's the untold stories of pioneering players, the rich tapestry of college football, or the globalization of the sport, these uncharted territories represent untapped potential for filmmakers to capture and audiences to experience.

Changing Societal Dynamics:

Football, like any cultural phenomenon, is deeply intertwined with societal dynamics. The conclusion explores how future films could reflect and dissect the evolving sociocultural landscape surrounding football. Questions related to gender representation, diversity, and the impact of football on communities are highlighted as potential areas of exploration. As societal attitudes shift, the films of tomorrow may become powerful tools for introspection and discussion on broader social issues.

Technological Advancements in Filmmaking:

The world of cinema is constantly evolving, driven by technological advancements that open new possibilities for storytelling. The conclusion speculates on how future filmmakers might leverage emerging technologies, such as virtual reality, augmented reality, and advanced visual effects, to immerse audiences in the visceral experience of football. The analysis considers the potential for innovative storytelling techniques that could redefine the boundaries of sports filmmaking.

International Perspectives:

While American football has a dedicated and passionate following in the United States, the global appeal of the sport continues to grow. The conclusion contemplates how future films could explore the internationalization of football, capturing the stories of players, fans, and communities around the world. It considers the potential for cross-cultural collaborations and the impact of football as a global cultural phenomenon.

The Intersection of Football and Other Genres:

Football's storytelling potential extends beyond the realm of traditional sports films. The conclusion explores how future filmmakers might experiment with genre-blending, incorporating elements of comedy, drama, science fiction, or even fantasy into football narratives. It contemplates the potential for films that use football as a backdrop to explore broader themes, transcending the boundaries of the sports genre.

Fan Engagement and Interactive Storytelling:

In the age of digital connectivity, the relationship between filmmakers and audiences is evolving. The conclusion speculates on the potential for interactive storytelling experiences that engage fans in new and immersive ways. Whether through interactive documentaries, virtual reality experiences, or fan-driven narratives, the analysis envisions a future where football films become participatory journeys for audiences.

Ethical Considerations in Football Storytelling:

Football, like any sport, has its share of controversies, scandals, and ethical dilemmas. The conclusion raises questions about how future filmmakers will navigate these complex issues. It explores the potential for films that delve into the ethical considerations surrounding player safety, the impact of the sport on mental health, and the broader societal implications of football culture.

Impact Beyond the Screen:

While this book primarily explores the impact of football films on cinematic storytelling, the conclusion contemplates the broader influence of these films beyond the screen. It considers how football films can shape public perception, influence policy discussions, and contribute to larger societal conversations. The analysis speculates on the potential for films to catalyze positive change within the football community and society at large.

Collaborations Between Filmmakers and the NFL:

As the relationship between the NFL and filmmakers continues to evolve, the conclusion explores potential collaborations that could shape the future of football storytelling. It contemplates how partnerships between the league and filmmakers might lead to unprecedented access, innovative storytelling formats, and a deeper integration of the cinematic experience with the live spectacle of football.

Conclusion: A Continuum of Exploration

In wrapping up the discussion on lingering questions and avenues for future study, the conclusion emphasizes that the exploration of football on the silver screen is a continuum. The cinematic journey through the NFL is a dynamic narrative that reflects the ever-changing nature of both sport and storytelling. As filmmakers continue to peel back the layers of this intricate tapestry, new questions will arise, and new avenues for exploration will present themselves. The conclusion serves as an invitation for future scholars, filmmakers, and enthusiasts to embark on their own journeys, contributing to the rich and evolving discourse on the intersection of football and cinema.

### The Ever-Expanding Relationship of Film and Football

As the final whistle blows on this exploration of football's cinematic landscape, the conclusion turns its gaze to the ever-expanding and symbiotic relationship between film and football. This concluding chapter reflects on the dynamic interplay between these two cultural juggernauts, tracing the evolution of their connection and pondering the future trajectories that lie ahead.

### The Early Days: A Kickoff in Cinematic History

The cinematic journey of football began in the early days of film, with grainy footage capturing the rudimentary aspects of the game. The conclusion harks back to the birth of this relationship, highlighting how these early depictions laid the foundation for what would become a profound and enduring connection. From the silent films that showcased football's physicality to the newsreels that brought the gridiron to life, the analysis celebrates the humble beginnings of a partnership that would evolve into a multimedia phenomenon.

### Football Films as Cultural Time Capsules

As the decades unfolded, football films became more than just representations of the game—they became cultural time capsules. The conclusion delves into how football films mirror the societal shifts, technological advancements, and evolving norms of their respective eras. From the stoic heroism of mid-20th-century films to the nuanced narratives of the modern era, each film reflects not only the state of football but also the pulse of the times in which it was created.

### The Emergence of NFL Films: A Cinematic Revolution

A pivotal moment in the relationship between film and football was the emergence of NFL Films. The conclusion explores how the Sabol family's visionary approach transformed the way football was presented on screen. It delves into the cinematic techniques, dramatic storytelling, and artistic flourishes that became the hallmark of NFL Films. This section celebrates how the Sabols elevated football from a mere sport to a visual and emotional spectacle, forever changing the way audiences engaged with the game.

Hollywood's Love Affair with Football Stars

As Hollywood embraced football as a source of compelling narratives, a new dimension of the relationship emerged—the elevation of football stars to cinematic icons. The conclusion discusses how athletes like Jim Brown, Burt Reynolds, and O.J. Simpson transitioned from the gridiron to the silver screen, bringing their charisma and athleticism to Hollywood productions. It reflects on the impact of these crossovers, both on the athletes' careers and on the public's perception of football players as cultural figures.

Football's Influence on Film Genres

The relationship between film and football isn't confined to traditional sports dramas. The conclusion explores how football has seeped into various film genres, from comedies like "The Waterboy" to intense dramas like "Concussion." It reflects on the versatility of football as a storytelling device, transcending its sports label to become a vehicle for exploring themes of teamwork, perseverance, and the human spirit.

The Rise of Documentary Filmmaking in Football

In recent years, documentary filmmaking has experienced a renaissance, and football has been a focal point of this resurgence. The conclusion analyzes the impact of documentary films like "Last Chance U" and "QB1: Beyond the Lights," exploring how these productions provide an unfiltered and intimate look at the lives of players, coaches, and the communities connected to football. It contemplates how the documentary format has become a powerful tool for humanizing the sport.

Football as a Reflection of Society's Complexities

Beyond the spectacle of the game itself, football films have become a canvas for exploring the complexities of society. The conclusion reflects on how films like "Remember the Titans" and "Friday Night Lights" tackle issues of race, identity, and community, using football as a lens to examine broader societal challenges. It considers how these narratives contribute to ongoing conversations about inclusivity, representation, and social justice.

The Globalization of Football Cinema

As football's popularity transcends borders, the relationship between film and the sport has become increasingly global. The conclusion explores how international filmmakers have depicted football in diverse cultural contexts, from the Brazilian favelas in "City of God" to the English working-class neighborhoods in "The Damned United." It contemplates how these films contribute to a more nuanced and interconnected understanding of football's global impact.

Technology and the Immersive Football Experience

Advancements in technology have not only enhanced the visual spectacle of football but also transformed the cinematic experience. The conclusion discusses how innovations like high-definition broadcasts, virtual reality, and augmented reality have elevated the way audiences engage with football on screen. It contemplates the potential for future technologies to further blur the lines between the live experience and cinematic storytelling.

The Streaming Revolution: A New Era for Football Films

The advent of streaming platforms has ushered in a new era for football films, providing unprecedented access and distribution channels. The conclusion explores how platforms like Netflix, Amazon Prime, and others have become crucial players in the dissemination of football-related content. It reflects on the democratization of football narratives, allowing fans around the world to access a diverse array of stories and perspectives.

Fan Engagement and the Participatory Experience

In the age of social media and digital connectivity, the conclusion considers the evolving nature of fan engagement. It reflects on how fans are not merely passive consumers but active participants in the dialogue surrounding football films. From online forums to fan-generated content, the analysis contemplates how the relationship between filmmakers and audiences has become more dynamic, fostering a sense of community and shared storytelling.

The Future of Football Cinema: Uncharted Territories

As the conclusion looks to the future, it contemplates the uncharted territories that lie ahead in the relationship between film and football. It raises questions about how emerging technologies, societal shifts, and the evolving nature of the sport itself will shape the narratives yet to be told. It encourages filmmakers, scholars, and enthusiasts to embark on new journeys, exploring the ever-expanding landscape of football's cinematic universe.

Conclusion: A Dynamic and Enduring Partnership

In closing, the conclusion celebrates the dynamic and enduring partnership between film and football. From the earliest cinematic depictions to the modern era of streaming, this relationship has evolved, adapted, and enriched the cultural tapestry of both mediums. As the credits roll on this exploration, the analysis acknowledges that the ever-expanding relationship between film and football is a testament to the enduring power of storytelling and the indelible mark that this beloved sport has left on the silver screen. The cinematic journey continues, and the ball is still in play, waiting for new stories to unfold.

**THE END**

**Glossary**

Here are some key terms and definitions related to AI-driven cryptocurrency investing:

1. Silver Screen Legends: Refers to iconic figures and stories in cinema, emphasizing the legendary status of certain films and individuals within the medium.

2. NFL Films: The official filmmaking arm of the National Football League, producing documentaries and highlight reels to capture the drama and spectacle of American football.

3. Football Cinema: A genre of film that revolves around the sport of football, encompassing various styles and approaches to storytelling within the context of the game.

4. Evolution of Football on Screen: The gradual development and transformation of how football is portrayed in cinematic narratives, reflecting changes in storytelling, technology, and cultural perspectives.

5. Iconic NFL Movies: Films that have achieved legendary status in the realm of football cinema, known for their impact on the genre and their lasting influence on audiences.

6. Themes and Comparisons: Common motifs and narrative elements explored across multiple NFL films, allowing for comparisons that reveal deeper insights into storytelling trends and thematic choices.

7. Masculinity and Rebellion: Key thematic elements often explored in football films, examining the concepts of

masculinity and rebellion against societal norms within the context of the sport.

8. Underdog Tale: A recurring narrative archetype in football cinema where a seemingly disadvantaged or underestimated individual or team overcomes challenges to achieve success.

9. Cinematic Flourishes: Artistic and stylistic techniques employed by filmmakers to enhance the visual and emotional impact of football scenes, contributing to the overall cinematic experience.

10. Cultural Impact: The influence that NFL films and football cinema have on broader culture, shaping public perception, influencing discussions, and leaving a lasting mark on societal attitudes toward the sport.

11. Streaming Platforms: Digital services like Netflix and Amazon Prime that provide online access to a wide range of football-related content, contributing to the changing landscape of football film distribution.

12. Fan Engagement: The active involvement of football enthusiasts in discussions, creation of content, and sharing of experiences related to football cinema, facilitated by online platforms and social media.

13. Globalization of Football: The process by which football has become a worldwide phenomenon, influencing filmmaking in diverse cultural contexts and contributing to a more interconnected understanding of the sport.

14. Documentary Filmmaking: A genre of filmmaking that presents real-life events and narratives, exploring the lives

of players, coaches, and communities connected to football in an unfiltered and intimate manner.

15. Technology in Football Films: The integration of technological advancements, such as high-definition broadcasts, virtual reality, and augmented reality, to enhance the visual and immersive aspects of football storytelling on screen.

16. Streaming Revolution: The shift in how football films are distributed and consumed, with streaming platforms playing a pivotal role in making diverse football narratives accessible to global audiences.

17. Participatory Experience: The interactive and dynamic nature of fan engagement with football films, where fans actively contribute to discussions, create content, and shape the narrative around the sport.

18. Uncharted Territories: Future possibilities and undiscovered themes or narratives within football cinema that remain untapped, representing potential avenues for exploration by filmmakers and scholars.

## Potential References

In addition to the content presented in this book, we have compiled a list of supplementary materials that can provide further insights and information on the topics covered. These resources include books, articles, websites, and other materials that were used as references throughout the writing process. We encourage you to explore these materials to deepen your understanding and continue your learning journey. Below is a list of the supplementary materials organized by chapter/topic for your convenience.

Introduction:

No specific references are provided for the introduction, as it serves as an overview and does not draw on specific external sources.

Chapter 1 - The Longest Yard (1974):

Albert, J. (Director). (1974). The Longest Yard [Motion picture]. Paramount Pictures.

Chapter 2 - North Dallas Forty (1979):

Kotcheff, T. (Director). (1979). North Dallas Forty [Motion picture]. Paramount Pictures.

Chapter 3 - Brian's Song (1971):

Sargent, B. (Director). (1971). Brian's Song [Television film]. ABC Circle Films.

Chapter 4 - Rudy (1993):

Anspaugh, D. (Director). (1993). Rudy [Motion picture]. TriStar Pictures.

Chapter 5 - The Replacements (2000):

Falstein, H. (Director). (2000). The Replacements [Motion picture]. Warner Bros. Pictures.

Chapter 6 - Any Given Sunday (1999):

Stone, O. (Director). (1999). Any Given Sunday [Motion picture]. Warner Bros.

Chapter 7 - The Blind Side (2009):

Hancock, J. L. (Director). (2009). The Blind Side [Motion picture]. Warner Bros.

Chapter 8 - Invincible (2006):

Core, E. (Director). (2006). Invincible [Motion picture]. Walt Disney Studios Motion Pictures.

Chapter 9 - Jerry Maguire (1996):

Crowe, C. (Director). (1996). Jerry Maguire [Motion picture]. TriStar Pictures.

Chapter 10 - Draft Day (2014):

Reitman, I. (Director). (2014). Draft Day [Motion picture]. Summit Entertainment.

Chapter 11 - Themes and Comparisons Across the Films:

Murray, N., & Rosenthal, A. (Producers). (2011). A Football Life [Television series]. NFL Films.

Chapter 12 - NFL Films' Impact on Wider Culture:

Sabol, S., & Sabol, S. (Producers). (1962-present). NFL Films [Film production company]. NFL Films.

Conclusion:

No specific references are provided for the conclusion, as it serves as a summary and does not draw on specific external sources.

www.ingramcontent.com/pod-product-compliance
Lightning Source LLC
LaVergne TN
LVHW012034070526
838202LV00056B/5498